The Concise Guide to TRACING YOUR ANCESTRY

Brian Loomes

929.1072 L873   ✓   MAR. 9 4
Loomes, Brian.
The concise guide to tracing
 your ancestry   22.95

MID-CONTINENT PUBLIC LIBRARY

Parkville Branch
Parkville Heights Shopping Ctr.
8815 NW 45 Highway
Parkville, MO 64152   **PV**

BARRIE & JENKINS
LONDON

OTHER REFERENCE BOOKS BY BRIAN LOOMES

Antique British Clocks: A Buyer's Guide
British Clocks Illustrated
The Concise Guide to British Clocks
Complete British Clocks
Country Clocks and their London Origins
The Early Clockmakers of Great Britain
Grandfather Clocks and their Cases
Lancashire Clocks and Clockmakers
Westmorland Clocks and Clockmakers
White Dial Clocks, the Complete Guide
Yorkshire Clockmakers

First published in Great Britain in 1992 by
Barrie & Jenkins Ltd
20 Vauxhall Bridge Road, London SW1V 2SA

Copyright © Brian Loomes 1992

All rights reserved. No part of this publication may be reproduced, stored
in a retrieval system, or transmitted in any form or by any means,
electronic, mechanical, photocopying, recording or otherwise, without
prior permission in writing from the publishers.

Brian Loomes has asserted his right to be
identified as the author of this work.

A catalgoue record for this book is available
from the British Library.

ISBN 0 7126 9877 9

Designed by Behram Kapadia
Documents on front cover by courtesy of
The Pitstone Local History Society
Typeset by Edna A Moore, 🖝 Tek-Art, Addiscombe, Croydon, Surrey
Printed and bound in England by Clays Ltd, St Ives, plc

MID-CONTINENT PUBLIC LIBRARY

3 0000 11097007 0

CONTENTS

MID-CONTINENT PUBLIC LIBRARY

Parkville Branch
Parkville Heights Shopping Ctr.
8815 NW 45 Highway
Parkville, MO 64152

PV

Foreword

Genealogy is one of today's fastest-growing leisure pursuits. Thousands of people worldwide find the quest of tracing their family origins both fascinating and satisfying. Many more would be inclined to take up the ancestry trail if only they knew how to go about it. This Concise Guide aims to steer the beginner along the main avenues of approach, which are not really difficult to follow once you know how.

For many years I worked as a professional genealogist, having first begun by tracing my own male ancestry as a hobby. Most professionals tend to specialise in a particular region (in my case Yorkshire) and many of the examples I have used to illustrate certain types of record have been drawn from my own family research, others from Yorkshire records, others from genealogical documents concerning clockmakers of the past, the latter being my main interest today.

In the text, where I have often referred to 'he' and 'him', I do, of course, mean 'she' and 'her' equally. As it would be too cumbersome to spell it out every time, I hope this will be understood by all readers.

The parish map of Warwickshire is one of a series edited in the Atlas and Index of Parish Registers by Cecil Humphery-Smith, FSA, and appears by kind permission of the Trustees of the Institute of Heraldic and Genealogical Studies. Acknowledgement is due to the Registrar of the Diocese of Leicester and the Leicestershire Record Office for permission to reproduce the Marriage Allegation and Bond of Randel Loomes; to the Chief Clerk, Leicester Probate Sub-Registry and the Leicestershire Record Office for permission to quote extracts from the wills of Thomas Loomes and John Looms; to the Rt Revd Ian Harland, Bishop of Carlisle, and the Cumbria Record Office, Carlisle, for permission to reproduce probate documents of Daniel Ismay of Waverton, Guy Sanderson of Wigton and John Ismay of Westward, and the settlement certificate of Jane Ismay; and to Eaton Socon Parish Records and Bedfordshire County Record Office for permission to publish the Examination and Removal Papers of Eden Wadsworth.

Pateley Bridge   *Brian Loomes*
North Yorkshire
1992

INTRODUCTION

Most of us at some time or other are intrigued to know who our ancestors were. Where did they live? What did they do? How far back did they go? Were they famous or unknown, rich or poor? The questions are endless. Some can be answered, some can not.

Many who wonder about their family origins do no more than that, principally because they don't know how to go about it. Some who make a start at tracing their ancestry fall by the wayside early in the quest; they get bogged down in the first stages, usually because they have gone about it in the wrong way.

Those who do have some success, however, make an amazing discovery: they find that the historical detective work of genealogy can be a fascinating pursuit for its own sake. What they expected to be an interest of only a week or two can turn out to be a lifetime's hobby. Many dedicated genealogists, including a large number of today's professionals, began with only a casual interest.

That is what happened to me. I began by looking into the origins of my own family. An uncommon surname like Loomes is, of course, a great help as there are comparatively few of them and fewer false trails to ensnare one. However, having traced my own family back to the late sixteenth century, I found I enjoyed the research for its own sake and didn't want to stop. I began to help others research their origins, at first on a semi-professional footing as a record searcher, then, ultimately, as a full-time professional genealogist.

During the years I was a professional I learned something which may surprise the beginner. I found I could often trace a family history more successfully and at lower cost than could a novice attempting to do it for himself. The reason is that the novice wastes much time and incurs expense looking for the wrong information in the wrong place. The professional knows exactly what to do and where to go, so can move both quickly and economically.

However, to the independent researcher, moving quickly is not the most important objective; the principal objective is the quest itself, and this should be its own chief pleasure. Each research trail of family history has its unique character and fascination, but it can only be savoured to the full, in a specifically personal way, if it is one's own family. Not only that but, as research progresses, unexpected offshoots of discovery are thrown up, many of which are only of particular interest to the family concerned. It is this sense of personal involvement and excitement that is the best reason why you should embark upon the quest yourself and do all, or most of, the research. You can always call for professional help when you need it. To most people someone else's family tree can be very boring, but the professional will regard your family tree with the same enthusiasm as he would his own and he'll find considerable pleasure and satisfaction in achieving a successful outcome.

PLAN YOUR CAMPAIGN

When you have decided upon tracing your family history your foremost task, to which all others are subordinate, must be to plan your campaign with as much care and thought as a general planning a battle. You will acquire, sift and assimilate facts and figures, draw up diagrams to show relationships, and begin to form your pedigree chart. This is also the most satisfying and enjoyable part, and by far the most vital. Any errors in this initial preparation will cause you to waste time, money and effort in following false trails, some of which might even result in your losing track of your ancestors' origins for ever: you will come to a dead end and will not know the way out and on, therefore you may conclude there is no way and give up. When planning your campaign you must bear in mind two very important things.

The sequence of research

The first essential is to start at the beginning. There is a set sequence of steps to be taken which varies little whatever the family. If the beginner does not know these, he will often begin at the wrong point and follow dead-end paths to failure. Frequently he will try to begin at a point too far back, where his information is imprecise or even inaccurate, and in doing so may miss vital clues which would steer him along the right track.

In this book I shall set out for you the basic steps of research procedure and their correct sequence. They are explained in detail so that you can learn and understand them, and can refer back to them whenever you need.

Location of records

The second essential you must work upon from the beginning is to determine the specific records you will need to search, and discover where they are kept. Until you know their correct locations, you will be wasting your time and money, as well as those of other people, such as staff of record offices. This book gives you full explanations of the various categories of records you are likely to have to use, how to use them, and where to find them. It also gives guidance on tracking down the more unusual kinds of document you might have to look at.

EXAMINING THE RECORDS

There has been a tremendous increase of interest in local history and genealogy over the last thirty years, mostly from people of comparatively humble origins who discovered the fascination of tracing their ancestry. Before then, most of the interest came from titled or monied families, thus County Record Offices and other archives repositories were often places of undisturbed tranquillity. Staff often saw their function as preserving ancient documents which were rarely looked at by anyone except archivists. In the early 1960s, when my interest first began, record office staff often regarded requests from people like me, for sight of anything as mundane as a parish register, as little better than a waste of time – 'misdirected enthusiasm' one of them called it. But if they were sometimes hostile to the private researcher, they were doubly so towards professionals, presumably because professionals were paid to use the records the archivists were paid to preserve.

Now the situation is quite different; attitudes, for the most part, have changed. With the great upsurge of public interest in local history and genealogy in recent years, researchers – private and professional – usually meet with helpful responses from staff. Inevitably this new popularity has also brought about considerable congestion in record offices, which means it is always best to make a prior appointment when you plan a visit. Telephone or write first. If you just arrive on the doorstep at 9.30am without warning, you may well be turned away for lack of space.

Once inside the record office you must know exactly what you are looking for and go straight to it. Again, pre-planning is essential; your time there is limited therefore precious. Your immediate task is to write in your notebook, as quickly as possible, everything which might relate to your family. Copy it just as you see it, and do not, at this stage, attempt to make sense of all the jottings; there will be plenty of time to do that at home later.

Of course, it is bound to happen that sometimes you will have to re-visit a record office and look at the same records again because you later realised they contained further information of which the importance was not apparent on your first visit. Careful pre-planning will reduce the likelihood of this happening, but it can't totally rule it out.

INTERPRETING DOCUMENTS

One problem that is likely to concern you is that you may encounter records in ancient scripts that you cannot read or cannot understand – or both. This is not the insuperable difficulty it may seem.

All the documents you will need fall into general categories. Once a document's category is known, its function, purpose and content can be identified, and its details become relatively easy to interpret. The book gives you detailed information on all categories of documents you are likely to encounter, with full discussion on their uses and general locations of store. Of course, if you were to attempt to read, say, a text in sixteenth-century English handwriting, having no prior experience, it could well defeat you. But in practice you will not do that: you will work your way back through documents which you *can* read so that you gradually become accustomed to changing styles, both in calligraphy and in forms expression. By the time you are three or four hundred years back into your family history you will be sufficiently familiar with script styles and terminology – the officialese, or jargon, of the time – to find that the original problem has virtually solved itself.

What if the document is in Latin and you have no Latin at all? Here, as with English texts, document categories are of prime importance. Once you know the category, you will also know the document's function and content. As for the details, you will recognise proper names, and such Latin as is generally used has its own set phraseology. When you have met and understood one such document in a category, you will instantly recognise another and will find subsequent ones comparatively easy to interpret. Anyway, documents you are likely to meet which contain Latin are all explained in the book.

THE PROFESSIONALS

You should bear in mind that the help of professionals can be at hand if you want it, or if you need assistance with a certain aspect of research. For instance, you may discover that a particular archive is a long distance away. Unless you have a specific reason for wanting to go yourself, it nearly always makes sense to seek the help of a specialist record searcher in the area. He or she can do it quickly and efficiently, thus saving you time, as well as the expense and hassle of travelling.

In any event, if you are serious about your research, one of your first steps should be to contact the **Society of Genealogists**. This is a non-profitmaking society which exists to 'promote and encourage' the study of genealogy, local history and heraldry. Its primary function is to help amateurs, and during the recent years of genealogy's rapid growth in popularity – and long before, of course – it has been a haven of help, support and encouragement to many beginners.

The Society publishes leaflets covering all topics necessary to the beginner. It also issues a quarterly publication, the 'Genealogists' Magazine', which includes advertisements from professional researchers in various parts of the country, which could be invaluable to you. At its London headquarters it has a vast document collection, transcripts of originals, copies of records in typescript, manuscript and microfilm. Its huge library includes virtually all published family histories, as well as such volumes as Burke's *Family Index*, and *Genealogical Research Directory* and the *National Genealogical Directory*. It also publishes its own books of scholarly research in individual subject areas, but they are specialist volumes, not for the absolute beginner.

(Books that will be of use to you now and in the future are listed in the bibliography in Appendix D (page 182)).

The Society of Genealogists has its own research department through which it is able to conduct research on a professional basis, depending on its work load at any given time. It also maintains a card index of members' interests, which could enable you to make useful contacts and see what others are doing. That would be especially important if someone else were currently researching another branch of your family; you would thus be saved much work. Write to the Society and ask them to send you details of membership and the facilities offered, enclosing a large stamped addressed envelope. Their address is:

> The Society of Genealogists
> 14 Charterhouse Buildings
> Goswell Road
> London EC1M 7BA
> Telephone: 071-251 8799

Another organisation that is of importance to you is the **Federation of Family History Societies** whose purpose is to co-ordinate the activities of various local family history groups. They have a host of member societies based in most counties of the British Isles and there are over 150 member societies world-wide. The Federation publishes numerous booklets detailing the where-abouts of particular categories of records. It also issues a six-monthly magazine, 'Family History News and Digest'. Write to them sending a large stamped addressed envelope.

> The Federation of Family History Societies
> c/o The Benson Room
> Birmingham and Midland Institute
> Margaret Street
> Birmingham B3 3BS

Many enthusiasts today belong to groups which investigate single surnames. These are known as One-Name Groups and they are formed within the **Guild of One-Name Studies**, an association through which one or more people interested in the history of a particular surname can combine with others to record all instances of that surname. As a beginner you may not be interested in joining, or forming, such a society, but later on you might be. On the other hand it could be worth your while to see if your surname is among those being studied, then contact the appropriate group with a view to exchanging information. The Guild publishes a *Register of One-Name Studies* which lists names and addresses of Guild members, and also *Record Keeping for a One-Name Study*. Contact the Guild to get their list of names currently under investigation, and other literature, enclosing a stamped addressed envelope:

> The Guild of One-Name Studies
> PO Box G
> 14 Charterhouse Buildings
> Goswell Road
> London EC1M 7BA

Addresses of other professional organisations are given in Appendix B (page 173).

HOW FAR BACK CAN YOU GO?

What can you reasonably expect to achieve in tracing your family back to its origins? How far can you go? This largely depends upon the family. If it was wealthy it will probably be easier to trace because its members will have left behind them a profusion of documents which that wealth involved – wills and other legal papers; documents of land purchase, ownership, sale; documents concerning property of all kinds, and much else. Moreover, a wealthy family may have been long resident in a particular house or parish. Their sons will have been through schools, colleges, universities, the army or the clergy . . . all places where their names can be tracked down in the records. With such plentiful documentation the family genealogy should be less of a problem and you can probably go back a long way – as far back as records of a genealogical nature and fixed surnames survive.

A family with an uncommon surname also has a great advantage as the records you can collect of that name will be fewer in number, more localised in area and less confusing to sort out. How far back you can go depends on many other factors.

But let us suppose your name, like most, is neither rare nor commonplace. Let us also suppose that you did not have wealthy ancestors. What is reasonable to expect?

Many English families can be traced without real problems to the mid-17th century. During the Civil War (1640–1660) certain records were sometimes badly kept, sometimes not kept at all, and even the best of them were patchy. To get beyond this period you need considerable luck. You may find your ancestors were, at this time, living in a parish where earlier registers have been lost, in which case you would seem to have an insurmountable problem. Of course you may be even more unfortunate and find that in 'your' parish of interest the registers do not go back beyond the 19th century. That is unusual, but it does occur.

From the latter part of the 18th century the Industrial Revolution began to draw increasingly large populations into towns from the countryside. Prior to this, the bulk of the population worked either in agriculture or in agriculture-based trades such as carpentry, smithing, wheelwrighting, or in other trades which arose from, or because of, agriculture.

By the time you have traced your ancestry back to the late 18th century the chances are that you discover your family resided within less than a twenty-mile radius as far back as you can hope to go – which, if you are fortunate, might be to about 1600. To expect to trace them back beyond that time is optimistic, to say the least – through it can happen.

As you progress in your research, you will have to draw and redraw your family tree many times as evidence mounts up.

Relationships you first believed absolute may now prove not to exist, or to be more complicated than first imagined, and new forebears constantly appear on the scene. But this is the thrill of research, and most exciting of all is the fact that you are uncovering *your* family history for the first time ever. The sooner you start the better, and I wish you luck and all the joy of the chase.

1 MAKING A START

There are many reasons why you could want to investigate your family origins and, whichever one it is, it will to some extent affect the line of procedure you take – although you will basically follow the set sequence of research steps we shall be looking at shortly.

For instance, you may have an unusual surname and want to discover where it came from; you may want to know more about your antecedents generally; you may want to investigate family legends that you are related to a famous person or a noble family, or you may want to trace a long-lost relative. There could be plenty of other reasons too, but let us comment briefly on each of those mentioned. We shall be discussing them in detail in other parts of the book.

SOME REASONS FOR INVESTIGATING YOUR ANCESTRY

Surnames Following a surname is done by pursuing the male line back in time (or it can be done through the female surname if preferred). It is the most straightforward of the processes, one that is much used, and probably best for the beginner. Genealogists normally work backwards a step at a time, from the known to the unknown, proving each link in a family chain as they go. Only in one exceptional circumstance (see below) do they start in the past and work forward.

Antecedents generally Here we branch into both male and female names at each generation, working backwards, following four names of grandparents, eight of great-grandparents and so on, the number doubling at each generation. This is more complicated than pursuing just the male line because you are trying to memorise relationships and keep records of an ever-increasing number of families at the same time.

Famous relations? Whatever legends run in your family, it is only fair to warn you that the majority of ancestral claims to fame and nobility are groundless. But it's always worth a try, and here you work from your own known ancestors back in time again. Never try to do it the other way round. If, for instance, you are called Washington and believe you are related to the great George, you don't look up the genealogy of George Washington in a reference book and hope to steer your own line back to link in with it. Worse still would be to assume you descend from his second cousin and start to work forward from that cousin towards the present day. If you do, you will almost certainly find you have enlarged George Washington's pedigree only to discover that it fails to meet up with any link in your own.

Long-lost relatives The task of tracing present-day descendants of a family is often as much detective work as genealogy, but it arises regularly when someone dies intestate and solicitors have a duty to search out missing heirs, or others who might inherit.

This is the one case of exception to genealogists' general rule of working backwards in time: here we fix upon a known date in family history as a starting point and work forwards from it, using the same records as for all normal research, but eventually coming to present-day electoral rolls, telephone directories and other such contemporary records.

This is a very specialised type of genealogy and one you are unlikely to be involved in unless you really do want to trace a long-lost distant relative or his issue.

I used to take on this kind of work when I was a professional. I remember one case where an elderly spinster died in the 1970s. Not only had she no children of her own, but neither had her brothers and sisters, all dead, nor her uncles and aunts. In the end I had to go back to about 1810 and work forward down the lines of brothers and sisters of her grandfather in order to find living kin, some of whom were in Australia and Canada. Scores of relatives were eventually traced, and I assume they duly inherited. But, amazingly, not one of them had even heard of the deceased benefactor. (Even more amazingly not a single one ever wrote to express pleasure, gratitude – or even thanks! – for having inherited a legacy from a totally unknown source.)

As I said earlier, there is an acknowledged sequence of steps to genealogical research, and these apply whatever your object of achievement – whether you decide to pursue only the male line back in time, or both the male and female lines of each generation. I will list this sequence briefly now, so that you can see what it looks like, and get an idea of the pattern of work we shall be following. We will then discuss the practical approach to the first step of the sequence and the work of preparation that must be done. In the ensuing chapters we shall follow each main process in detail and put it into context as we go.

SEQUENCE OF STEPS: THE ORDER OF GENEALOGICAL RESEARCH

1. Assemble what facts you can from family knowledge and draw a preliminary pedigree sketch ('family tree').

2. Begin Civil Registration searches.

3. Carry out census searches.

4. Acquire a parish register map of your county of interest. (*Note*: you can only do this when you have ascertained which county your family lived in towards the end of the 18th century. See page 50.)

5. Contact the Federation of Family History Societies to see if a group exists in your area of interest. If it does, join it.

6. Begin parish register searches.

7. Search for marriage licences or banns books.

8. Search nonconformist registers if applicable.

9. Search for wills and administrations.

10. Return to 3, 4, 7, 8, or 9 as the need arises.

11. Turn to other sources if applicable – apprenticeships, naval or military records, poll books, directories, Quarter Sessions records, etc.

This sequence of steps may at first look like a considerable work programme, but you will be carrying it out one stage at a time and will find enjoyment and interest in each aspect. The amount of time and effort spent at each stage will vary with factors specific to your own family. Also when you know where to go, what to look for and how to approach the various record offices, the task becomes less formidable and the research easier and more accessible. It is important not to rush through any one stage, or to attempt any step until the previous ones have fully prepared you for it. Most important of all is step 1.

RECALLING FAMILY KNOWLEDGE AND MEMORABILIA
The whole process begins by your telling others in your family of your interest and intentions. Talk to them, especially the older ones – but give them prior warning that you are coming to see them. They will need time to start thinking about things, to get chests out of attics, boxes out of lofts and blow dust off ancient documents. Older ladies of the family, especially, are likely to have kept papers which may well go back as far as their grandparents, or even further. One of them may even know that someone researched the family tree years ago, or that cousin John has a mass of paperwork about it. If you like working with a tape recorder, it is a good idea to record the more important sessions, but make notes of the spelling of people's names, place names, dates of birth/death, and other facts of key importance; inaccurate spellings can have you wasting time looking things up under wrong initial letters, and chaos can ensue when you try to unravel spellings where dialect or local pronunciation is involved.

Old photographs, newspaper obituaries, correspondence, scrap-books, funeral receipts, medals, demobilisation papers, copies of wills, memorial cards, certificates of birth, marriage or death . . . these are the kinds of documents hoarded in most households, or kept by one elderly member of the family. If you are very lucky, a family Bible may even exist recording – as was traditional – births, baptisms (christenings) of children, sometimes for more than one generation.

Study and take notes (see page 19) from papers such as letters and official documents, and make liberal use of photocopiers if the document owners don't object.

Prepare your questions carefully, bearing in mind what you most need to know. For instance, where did the family come from? What sort of trades did they follow? Are there any distant kin no longer in contact? When did great-grandfather die, and how old was he?

This way you will be able to form some kind of picture of the family group as far back as memory extends. Memories, of course, are often faulty, and you must make allowance for that, but you will be given plenty of valuable pointers and will almost certainly get some firm dates and place names from which to begin your first search which, as you see from the sequence steps, will be in the records of Civil Registration (see page 26).

PEDIGREE SKETCHES

Make notes of all important facts, especially names, places and dates. Compile these by looking over your hand-written notes, listening to any tapes you've recorded, and sifting through papers, photographs and other memorabilia you have been lent or given. It is best to photocopy valuable originals and work from the copies; that way it doesn't matter if you scribble on them, spill coffee or damage them, whereas it would matter greatly if you damaged the originals.

When you have enough evidence to see the broad outlines of your family, you should draw your first diagram in the style of what is normally regarded as a 'family tree', but to the genealogist is a 'pedigree'. This pedigree sketch – the working drawing – will be the first of many because its make-up will change as your research progresses.

In Fig 1.1 you will see a simple pedigree sketch of the Peckover family. This is typical of the kind of preliminary pedigree that can be assembled from information culled from living relatives. Relationships are probably accurate, though some dates are vague. At this stage the vagueness does not matter because we shall focus onto one particular event and confirm its details precisely, after which we can move onto other events which we can then more closely estimate.

In the sketch you will see that at the top I have entered Sir Richard Peckover who can only be regarded as a tentative ancestor. Although he has the family surname, little is known about him and he may be totally unrelated. If you were researching the family you would ignore him altogether to begin with, indeed continue to ignore him until such time as you found a line of definite connection leading back – which might never happen. You can always include such tentative ancestors in your own chart if you wish, but mark the connection in dotted lines to show that they are unproven relationships.

In researching the Peckovers, we would begin by confirming the oldest fact for which the chart indicates we have adequate data: the birth of Leonard Peckover. We are told enough about him to

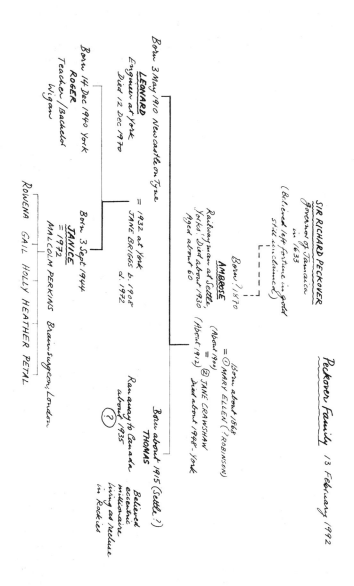

Fig. 1.1   *A simple pedigree sketch of the Peckover family.*

ensure that we could obtain a correct birth certificate. (We could not start with the marriage of Ambrose because we have inadequate information at this stage.)

This simple pedigree sketch is the kind you should start with. You can add to and alter the master copy as your research progresses.

In drawing up a pedigree sketch certain conventions are used. Give it a clear heading, with the date on which it was compiled. Keep one generation only to a line. Work from left to right in positioning children in seniority of birth. Space is cramped so use abbreviations where possible; these can be the same abbreviations as those used for note-taking (see page 22), except that 'married' is usually signified by an equals sign (=). More than one marriage of the same man is usually noted: = 1, = 2, or = 1st, = 2ndly. It is usual to separate children by a first wife from those by later wives by using a stroke (an oblique / through the horizontal line) to break the birth line between the issue of each wife. Incidentally, when a genealogical or heraldic artist draws up a finished pedigree sketch, he will have his own style of preferred abbreviations or symbols. These are usually obvious and will often be noted on the pedigree itself. For instance, on the finished pedigree on page 168 the symbol ★ means born, and † means died.

Join together as family groups only those people who are clearly related. You may well wish to draw up additional sketch pedigrees which involve guesswork, or suppositions showing possible relationships, but do this on a separate sheet of paper, using dotted lines where appropriate, and labelling them clearly as conjectural.

Draw your pedigree sketch so that you can understand it at a glance. If abbreviations are likely to confuse you, then write entries in such a way that their meaning is clear to you now and in the future. At the time you jot down your working sketches you will no doubt be quite certain in your own mind just what they mean. The problem is that when you look at them again months, or even years, later, you may have forgotten what you intended and be unable to read your writing. Anyone else trying to understand them might be even more baffled, and this would be a pity, especially if it were one of your own children trying to pick up on the research at some time in the future.

Fig. 1.2 is an example of a working sketch pedigree drawn from extracts from one search in the name of 'Sill' from the parish registers of Wigton, Cumberland, CMB (christenings, marriages and burials) 1660–1730.

'CMB', commonly used to indicate christenings (or baptisms, which are the same thing for genealogical purposes), marriages and burials, is used when referring to a parish register, or extract from one, though 'bap' is used when listing the entries. The double dates, '1710/11' indicate old and new style dating (see page 66). The burial of Janet describes her as 'f Richard Sill': 'f' is the

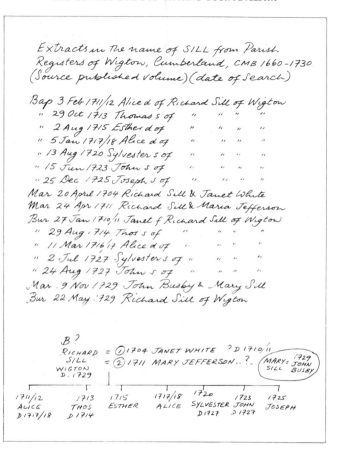

Fig. 1.2 *Extracts from parish register entries for the Sill family, and the pedigree sketch drawn up from it.*

abbreviation for 'filia', daughter, and is copied exactly as in the transcript. In fact Janet appears to be his wife, not daughter, and it looks as if the entry was a mistake of the clerk. (Checking in the originals and/or Bishop's Transcripts (BTs – see page 60) might confirm this.)

Richard Sill was one of the earliest Wigton clockmakers, though his trade is not mentioned in the registers. It seems that he had no children by his first wife, Janet, and that on her death in 1710/11 he remarried, three months later, Mary Jefferson (the Latin Maria was commonly used for Mary). The marriage of Mary Sill to John Busby in 1729 looks very much like the widow of Richard remarrying, but this is not certain so is sketched in by a dotted line as a separate, but possibly connected, item. Mary, whose baptism does not appear here, might even have been an earlier daughter of Richard, or a sister of Richard – or be totally unrelated. Later searches might clarify the position if, for example, any of the marriage licences could be traced.

For the present this sketch pedigree summarises what can reasonably be assumed from the entries, but some assumptions may later prove incorrect. For example, the 1704 marriage may have been that of a quite different Richard Sill from that of 1711. Although the sketches can only give at a glance the summarised position, they do offer many clues which may be helpful in later research. The daughters have not been named after either of his wives, and his apparent determination to have an Alice may indicate that this was his mother's name. Sylvester is an uncommon first name and may provide a clue to a relationship to another Sill family, found elsewhere, which may include a Sylvester.

The pedigree sketch is one of your most important working aids and it is important that you put small ones at the end of each page (or group of pages) of your notes, such as parish register extracts, will extracts, and anything else, so that they remain attached to the entries from which they were compiled. This will make more sense to you when we have discussed the note-making process generally.

NOTE-TAKING STAGE 1: NOTES FROM ORIGINAL SOURCES

When making your first notes from source, such as relatives' reminiscences, or original documents like parish registers, wills, or any other form of record, you will normally write in pencil on a notepad. The best is probably a ruled A4 with tearoff sheets, hole-punched, so that you can, if you wish, store them in a ring binder. Pencil is necessary because ink, including ball-points, is forbidden in most record offices, and you may as well get used to using it from the start.

Your first notes from source are the vital raw material of your search, but in this form they cannot be relied upon for long-term reference. This is only the preliminary stage in compiling the more permanent records, which you must do as soon as you get home – or as soon afterwards as possible.

In taking notes from record books you should always quote the entries in the exact wording in which they are written. If the entry doesn't look quite right to you, copy it all the same; you can puzzle over its ambiguities and exact meaning when you get home. (If you can't even fathom it then, copy the query onto your record page with the rest of the entries; its ambiguity may eventually become clear in the light of other findings.)

You will write your notes in the order in which you encounter the material from source – whether it is a person speaking, or documents to be copied from – and that order may not be the one in which you will ultimately wish to use it.

Also you will probably be writing quickly, even illegibly to anyone but yourself at the time. You must therefore transcribe these scribbles before the pencil blurs, your memory goes cold, and you can no longer read your own writing.

It happens only too easily. For instance you may be in the record office, switching between several registers, or working from different books within the same register. You are writing frantically, copying out baptisms and burials in your notebook. It may all make perfect sense to you at the time, but afterwards could be a different matter. If you allow the notes to lie untouched in your notebook for a few weeks – or even days – there is a fair chance that when you return to them you will no longer be certain about which are baptisms and which burials.

How can you avoid this confusion and convert your raw material into the permanent, technically correct records you need if you are accurately to reconstruct the historical record of your family?

NOTE-TAKING STAGE 2: COMPILING AND ORGANISING YOUR RECORDS

The system I suggest for your second stage of note-recording is based on the assumption that you will accumulate a great deal of paper as your research progresses. How quickly it amasses depends upon your objectives and your research areas: if you are pursuing one line only, such as the male line, the paper bulk should not become too formidable too quickly. For wider research, or in certain other instances – such as if you have a very common surname – you will expect be accommodate a huge amount of paper.

I have used a simple record system for many years, for a large number of researches and find it always works well. It will adequately cope with all your material and enable you easily to see the results of your investigations at any given moment. It also costs comparatively little.

You should acquire an A4 loose-leaf ring binder, and if you wish you can use marking cards to separate the different subject sections. This is to accommodate your second-stage notes which you type, print (from a word processor), or write clearly by hand, on A4 punched pages that match the binder. As you file these notes in their sections on a page by page basis, one binder should be enough to contain all you need, but if it does become full, it is easy to begin another and move sections of notes about as you wish.

Your method will be to extract and copy vital information from original documents – notes taken from relatives, extracts from parish registers, details from certificates of birth, marriage or death, and anything else – onto your punched pages and file them in the appropriate sections of the ring-leaf book. Label each section with the category of document whose details you are recording, such as Civil Registration, Census, Parish Register, Wills, and so on. The notes must be carefully prepared from your original jottings, and each entry given full identity, including its heading (name of document), source, date, and other relevant details.

If you are recording a search from a parish register, for example, put the heading at the top, as in Fig. 1.2, then the period covered and the surname. Note any missing or illegible years. If you did not find any appropriate entries, it is nevertheless important to record the search and its period, or you may risk repeating a fruitless search at some future time. However, negative results can often prove worth while later: they might, perhaps, be useful in showing the area of distribution of a name, which can point you in the direction of more fruitful parishes, probate jurisdictions, and so on. Of course, if you forgot to note which surname the search was for, you might later be uncertain whether you searched this record for just the male name or for the bride's ancestry too.

When you have extracted all vital information from your first rough notes, and any copy records and documents you may have, you can store away the original papers. I use box files, but you can use anything else you may prefer. Keep each category of document together, and annotate them clearly so that you know where they are and can identify them easily. Some you may never need again, but others may have to be examined a second time. As long as you know you can get at them quickly, you can now store them right away from your main working area.

The object of compiling these files of clear, well-prepared notes, fully annotated for reference, is to slim down the vast bulk of material you accumulate, leaving you with the essential hard facts you need. With superfluous matter excluded, there is an excellent chance that you will see connections, relationships and lines forward and back that you would not be able to see if you were up to the eyes in clutter.

I said earlier that each page of your ring-binder notes should carry a small pedigree sketch representing the situation at that point, as it relates to the content of that particular search page. It is important you do this and, at the same time, keep a larger master pedigree running separately. The master shows the summary of your own proven family tree, taken from such of the smaller pedigree sketches as do actually relate to your family, because it may well be that some of the rough, working sketches will prove to be pieces of other non-related but same-name families. You will update your master pedigree by adding new details as and when they occur.

Your system of organisation and filing can be as simple or as complicated as you like. Some people like to have an elaborate system with indexes that would do a librarian proud; others manage quite well with scribblings on the backs of envelopes. Most of us are somewhere in between.

Of course, if you use a computer/word processor you will be able to record and store material on disk as your findings progress. All kinds of possibilities are open to you, and you will doubtless devise your own methods.

(More about the use of computers for genealogical purposes is on page 171.)

With or without a computer you may like to follow the system used by some researchers who have a record card for each male ancestor on which is detailed his baptism, marriage, children, death, burial and tombstone inscription, plus anything else they can discover. I have never, myself, found this system particularly helpful, except when encountering a 'rogue' ancestor – one who is proving particularly obstinate. In such a case it is useful to set out all the facts about the 'rogue' on a single sheet, listing items found and items still missing.

One can also include all possible avenues of approach yet to be tried. Is it unlikely that this sort of problem will arise early in your research, but by the time it does, I hope that you will be sufficiently experienced to be able to work from your pedigree sketches – which will set out the problems more clearly than record cards.

Common abbreviations for note-taking

The time you spend in County Record Offices or other archives is valuable and, although you may have to make several visits as new information is revealed and your detective work progresses, you don't want to be compelled to re-visit because you can't understand the notes you made first time. We have stressed the importance of clear handwriting in your notebooks, but if you use a code of accepted abbreviations, you can save space on the page, and reduce the tedium of long sessions of copying.

The abbreviations that are commonly used by genealogists today, can be used all the time – in your first-stage notes, your second-stage record pages, and in your pedigree sketches (where brevity is of the essence). Here are the main ones:

Genealogical abbreviations

b	– born
bac(h)	– bachelor
bap	– baptised
bur	– buried
c.	– circa (about)
CMB	– christenings (baptisms), marriages and burials (in parish registers)
d	– died
dau	– daughter (sometime dtr, or d where obvious)
m (or marr.)	– married
o.t.p.	– of this parish
s	– son
w	– wife
wid	– widow
widr	– widower

As you see, there is an unfortunate proliferation of the letter b. Usually it stands for 'born', but don't use it carelessly as your own shorthand for 'baptised' or 'buried' because that will obviously lead to trouble. Use 'bap' or 'bur', the abbreviations given. In most dates before 1837, entries will generally be for baptisms not births.

In pedigree sketches of the past, *obit* (Latin for 'died') was frequently used, and o was its abbreviation. When you see 'o.s.p.' it means *obit sine prole*, died without issue.

An area of danger is in using abbreviations (especially your own) for entries in old records which are themselves abbreviated. Most of these old abbreviations are perfectly obvious, but if you are uncertain, copy the entry exactly as written. For instance Jo. could easily be open to misinterpretation, especially if inconsistently abbreviated by the clerk who wrote it. Is it short for John, Joseph or Jonathan? Again, copy it as it stands and leave decisions until later; the answer will usually be obvious from the context.

In taking notes, you may want to abbreviate certain well-known first names – though it's always safest to spell them out in full first time. For surnames you can use an abbreviation, or even the initial letter when the name is repeated, but again, spell it in full at first appearance.

You might well find an entry like

> William ye son of Richard Johnson of Langfield was baptised ye 20th June in ye same year (1748).

transcribed as

> Bap 20 Jun 1748 Wm. s. of Ric. J. of Langfield.

RESEARCH THAT OVERLAPS YOUR OWN

There is always a chance that someone may already have covered part of your research area before, working on the same surname. If this research was into your *own* family (perhaps done by a distant cousin) it is likely that you would already have learned about it during your initial inquiries among relatives. It is a slim chance but a possibility you should not ignore.

A stronger possibility is that someone may have investigated a family with your surname (perhaps even from the same locality as your family's), which might be connected with your own line at some point in the past. If this is so, you may not be in a position to recognise the connection early in your research, but it may become apparent when you have progressed two or three generations back.

It would therefore be very helpful if you could know of such research at an early stage, even though its true value may not be proved until later. Of course there is the chance that the research may turn out not to be of use to you at all – but it is as well to know about it.

There are several ways in which you can check on research that has already been done, or is currently in progress. Any large reference library, and of course specialist libraries such as that of the Society of Genealogists, will have a number of published volumes on family genealogies. These are perhaps better consulted at a later stage when you have added a few generations to your known genealogy.

A better way, at the early stages, is to consult those publications which summarise research which is currently in progress, and are revised annually. Past issues are also available and are fruitful sources of information.

The more uncommon your surname the greater your chances of discovering valuable overlapping research. With a common surname, your chances are less good, and may even be worthless. But supposing your name were Slatterthwaite and you made contact with someone else researching that name? It may be that although there is no apparent connection with your family, he may have done numerous searches that you would need to do yourself, such as compiling lists of probates in that surname from certain courts. If you could obtain this information, and be prepared to offer some of your own to him in exchange, it could benefit you considerably.

The names of the publications to look in are as follows:

> *The Genealogical Research Directory*,
> English agent Mrs E. Simpson
> 2 Stella Grove
> Tollerton
> Notts NG12 4EY

The National Genealogical Directory
Editor, I. L. Caley
Hill View
Mendip Road
Stoke St Michael
Somerset BA3 5JU

Family History Knowledge
publishers K. & T. Park
19 Penybryn
Mountain Ash
Mid-Glamorgan CF45 3BR

The Guild of One-Name Studies was mentioned in the Introduction (page 9) and could be of great help to you. You should ask them for their latest list of names under investigation.

When writing to any of these contacts, you should, as always, enclose a stamped addressed envelope.

AN UNUSUAL SURNAME

If your surname is very unusual, one other approach is available to you. Locate others of the same name through telephone directories and write to each asking if they know anything of their ancestry which may connect with yours. You may find that one or more have actually done some research into their ancestry and it could easily connect with yours. Many will express interest, and it is worth your while talking to them, though even the best memory of the valuable older members of families rarely goes back far enough to be of really substantial use to you. However, such a search will indicate the present-day distribution of the name, which may be an important clue in locating the area of origin of your own ancestors.

Recently I was talking to a man who had researched his family and written to everyone he could find with the same surname. He had been so overwhelmed by the response that he had collected his material and published a small booklet about his family history. Within six months he had sold over 500 copies.

As a beginner it would be over-ambitious for you to contemplate anything like that, but when you are reasonably advanced along the lines of establishing your family tree, you will be in a stronger position to discuss matters knowledgeably with others, and may even discover that some are your distant kin.

Now that we have dealt with step 1 of the order of genealogical research, and preliminary matters, we can turn to the research proper: step 2 searches into the records of Civil Registration.

2 CIVIL REGISTRATION OF BIRTHS, MARRIAGES AND DEATHS

Having set down on paper all you can muster from family memories you will now be able to sketch your first family pedigree, brief though it may be. You should begin research by confirming the oldest event of which you are certain, or reasonably certain. In practice this will mean obtaining confirmatory details of the oldest birth or marriage by means of a certificate. If you already have such a certificate, you should then search for the next earlier one. It is always safest to work back by certificates – certificates of birth, marriage of parents, birth of father, marriage of his parents, and so on. Death certificates are less helpful at this stage, and it is a mistake to attempt to search for a birth of an ancestor based on supposed age at death on such a certificate unless you also know the father's name and location. Because of this it may seem that you will need to begin much closer to the present day than you imagined. In fact this is all to the good, because you may well be about to start your research, not with the oldest date you can muster, but with a much more recent event which is a *known* fact. Supposing you can calculate, perhaps from an age at death, that your ancestor Samuel Ramsbottom was born about 1812 in the Manchester area, it would be very unwise of you to assume that this is accurate and to begin by searching for evidence of that birth. There are numerous reasons why this could be futile: ages at death are often unreliable; places of origin are seldom what memory recalls; and you may well discover several people of that name born about the right time in the right area, but you have then no means of recognising which one is your ancestor.

THE BEGINNING OF CIVIL REGISTRATION, 1837

For most families the place to start searching is in the records of birth, marriage (and perhaps of death), known as the system of Civil Registration, which began on 1 July 1837. For many reasons, which will become apparent as we progress, we want to pin down the family location *precisely* at some period between about 1840 and 1880 and to do this it is likely that you will use certificates of birth and/or marriage and/or death. Since 1837 there has been a legal requirement for every birth, marriage and death in England and Wales to be registered at the nearest registration office, where these records are kept to this day, and where they can be examined. The registrar was obliged to send a copy of each certificate to a central repository, then Somerset House, London, which meant that indexed information for the whole country was available in the one place.

Before the beginning of Civil Registration in 1837, a family might have had events such as birth, baptism or marriage recorded in the annals of any of the religious faiths that family may have followed. Some families may not have attended any place of worship at all, and others may have changed their faith on numerous occasions. The Civil Registration meant that henceforth all births, marriages and deaths were recorded, and very few escaped the system. It is true that sometimes a post-1837 search will fail to locate the required event, but that is usually because of mis-spelling or mis-indexing, not because it was not recorded.

If your starting point falls after 1 July 1837, your first step must be to confirm the accuracy of a registered event. You may already have an old certificate of birth, but these exist in short as well as full-length forms, and the short form gives only limited information, which is inadequate for your purpose.

YOUR FIRST SEARCH

Begin with the oldest certificate of birth or marriage that you have. We will consider death certificates in due course but these are less helpful at this stage. The information given in a full birth certificate will be sufficient to enable you to search for the marriage certificate of the parents. The information on a marriage certificate will contain enough detail for you to then make a search for the birth certificate of the father (or of course of the mother if that is the way you intend to proceed). You can then leapfrog in this manner – birth, marriage, birth, marriage – until you reach that point closest to 1837 from which you can proceed no further with Civil Registration records. At this point you have only the thinnest outline of a family tree, and you may well need to return to these records later – we will come to that shortly. But meantime that thin outline is all you want at this stage, so let us consider how you go about this initial run through Civil Registration records.

You can make searches in person by visiting the appropriate office, or you can request a search be made on your behalf by the staff in the department concerned, or you can employ a profess-ional record searcher (see page 165). Whichever method you adopt you will have to pay the search fees and, if you employ a record searcher, you will have to pay for his time and knowledge too.

If you know the area where the event took place you can make this search in the local Register Office (its address will be in your local library) or you can opt for the General Register Office at St Catherine's House, Kingsway, London WC8 6JP.

My personal preference is always to use the General Office, since its records cover the whole country. If you should be mistaken in the area where you believe the event took place, a search in the General Register Office would *still* locate it. At the Office, you or your agent, would not be allowed to examine the volumes of registers themselves, but you will have access to their indexes which are in quarterly volumes under the appropriate initial letter. Once the index throws up what appears to be the required entry, the officials will issue a certified copy of the original. With common surnames, several certified copies might need to be obtained before the right one is found, which is why the fullest possible detail is needed before the search is embarked upon. With a birth certificate the registered date may be some time after the actual birth, perhaps even a month or two, and that might mean searching an index for a later quarter.

There are times when it might be best to use the records of the local registry, but this is only advisable if you are reasonably confident of the area where the event took place. For instance the local registry might be preferable if the surname were a common one, when the proliferation of index entries at the General Register Office would make recognition of the correct one a problem, or the acquisition of numerous certified copies (in order to establish the correct one) prohibitively costly.

The local registry might also be preferable if a search at the General Register Office has failed to locate the desired item because of mis-indexing: possibly the registered name is different from the name used by the person later in life. For example, a search for John Arthur Crabtree's birth might fail if he had been registered as Arthur John Crabtree and had decided to invert his first names later. If he had been registered plain Arthur Crabtree a central search is even more likely to fail, and this could have happened if he had simply adopted the first name John later in life because he liked the sound of it. In these circumstances, which cannot be anticipated in advance, it is more likely that a local registry search will spot the required entry. This is simply because there will be far fewer Crabtree births at the recorded date, and in spite of the fact that you may have requested a search for a name that was, strictly-speaking, inaccurate.

From the early years of registration each district was under the control of the superintendent registrar. The districts were in turn divided into sub-districts, each in the control of a registrar. To find the address of a local registry office today you need only look in the appropriate telephone directory. If you cannot do this because of the distance, send a reply-paid letter to the central library of the major town of the area. This should produce the address you need, but if you happen to write to the wrong registry, they will more than likely pass it on to the right one holding the records. When you write to the local registry, keep your letter brief and to the point, yet be sure to include all the details you have relating to the birth (or whatever) to be traced, and inquire what search fee will be required to locate it. Do not enclose your family history, fascinating as it is to you. The chances are they won't feel the same way about it.

Another aid to locating the registry you need is a leaflet sold by the Society of Genealogists called 'District Register Offices in England and Wales'.

The birth certificate

Let us consider what information is to be found on a birth certificate, since this is not always as straightforward as it might at first appear. As well as the registration district and sub-district, the form will tell us the answers given by the informant, at the time of registration, to the following questions:

> When and where born
> Name, if any
> Sex
> Name and surname of father
> Name and maiden surname of mother
> Rank or profession of father
> Signature, description and residence of informant
> Date when registered
> Signature of registrar
> Baptismal name (if added after registration of birth)

The information given is not always accurate. The informant, who may not necessarily have been one of the parents, may have got some of the details wrong, may even have spelled the name wrongly, or invented information (for instance, to conceal illegitimacy), or may simply not have known the answer to some part of the questionnaire, and left the space blank.

The 'name, if any' item may seem puzzling, since surely everyone has a name? The point is that the name may not have been decided upon at the time of registration, in which case that box would be left blank. A searcher looking for the birth of an Alice Alsop and failing to find it, should therefore check at the end of the Alsop listings, where those unnamed would be listed – in other words check under 'Alsop, female'. This is one of the small deviations which a professional searcher would always look for, and you would be well advised to do so too when need arises.

The entry for a child born to unmarried parents might fail to state the name of the father – if for instance the informant did not know it or refused to give it. Illegitimacy may well crop up in many family histories. After 1875 the father's name is stated for an illegitimate child only if he attended with the mother to register the birth, and such a birth is then indexed under both surnames. For a child born to married parents, the index would not show the mother's surname before 1911, though the entry itself and resultant certificate would.

Even if you are reasonably certain, from information available in family papers, that your ancestor was born in a particular place and year, and to known parents, it is still best to begin your serious research by tracing the full birth registration details on the birth certificate and confirming the facts. The reason is, the certificate may reveal some additional or more precise information. For example, it will give an exact location, and you will need this before you can turn to other sources such as the census records. This will apply especially if your family lived in a large town, when you will be glad of the street address. Even if they lived in a small village you may be pleased to have the actual parish because, at this stage in particular, you will not know which place was a parish in its own right at the time and you will need that information before you can attempt to locate the whereabouts of the parish registers. The ancient parishes and boundaries can be very different from those of today. There are ways of finding out which church was a parish church and which was not, and we will come to those in Chapter 4. For the moment, however, you want every piece of factual information as your starting point.

The marriage certificate

Before you can attempt to trace the marriage of the parents you will need to know the mother's maiden name, and this will be shown on the birth certificate. Even if the mother's maiden name is known to you, you may find that she was a widow who had re-married, and this may well have been forgotten in the family's written records. Your Alice Alsop may prove to have been the daughter of John Alsop and Mary Alsop, late Robinson, formerly Jones. This means that the mother was born Mary Jones, married firstly to someone named Robinson, then married secondly, as a widow, to John Alsop. Unless you knew this you might well be searching in vain for the marriage of John Alsop to Mary Jones. It is vital therefore to check every detail as fully as possible, and always be prepared for the unexpected.

For many reasons a confirmatory birth certificate is the best point at which to start. Having traced the appropriate birth, you can then move on (backwards in fact) to look for the marriage of the parents. Again you need to know the full names of both parties, which in the case of a bride who was a widow, will mean the surname of her late husband. There are two indexes to be checked: one for the groom and one for the bride. When the reference given for one tallies with that for the other, you know you have the right marriage and can request the full certificate. After 1912 the index for husband or wife is cross-referenced with the partner, so that only one index needs to be consulted. The name entered for the bride would be her surname at the time of marriage of course; if she was a widow, then her late husband's name.

Below are imaginary details in the manner set out in a certificate of marriage. In addition to the date of the marriage, the registration district, and the name of the church or chapel where the ceremony was performed, we have:

Percival Sykes, of full age, widower, labourer, (at time of marriage, of) Wetherby, (father) Samuel Sykes, hatter

Mary Ann Womersley, of full age, spinster, servant, (at time of marriage, of) Wetherby, (father) —

In this connection 'of full age' means aged 21 or more – the two parties may have been in their sixties even, as no indication is given. The bride's father's name is here left blank. This might be because she did not know who her father was or, as happened sometimes with illegitimate children, perhaps she refused to say. It might be because her father was deceased, but this conclusion should not be assumed. Similarly the presence of the name of the groom's father, and his trade, is no confirmation that the father was alive at that time; the word 'deceased' was sometimes added, sometimes not.

Both parties then signed the document, and if they could not write this would be by means of a mark, usually a cross (X). Two witnesses also usually signed. The names of witnesses may be helpful clues, or they may not, but they should be kept in mind just in case. A witness who signed herself Elizabeth Sykes, may just have been the groom's sister or mother, or was perhaps totally unrelated.

Details on such a certificate cannot always be relied on, any more than they can in any other form of document. If Percival Sykes had been illegitimate and had not known the name of his father, he may have decided to give the name of his grandfather in order to avoid embarrassment, or he may even have invented a father's name. He may have wished to conceal his illegitimacy not only from the registrar but from his bride too. Although falsified information on a certificate is very unusual, the common exception is the concealment of illegitimacy, and that may not have been deliberate, but simply that the person writing out the certificate (the vicar for example) may have thought it appropriate to leave the space blank in those circumstances, or to insert a mother's name instead of a father's.

The death certificate

A death certificate can be among the most difficult of all Civil Registration events to locate, most often because you may have only the vaguest notion as to when the person died. This naturally involves searching a wider span of years and will probably also involve locating many possible death entries. If the name is a common one it may be impossible to determine which, if any of them, is your ancestor. For this reason it is sometimes best to postpone the search for a death certificate – at least for a while. In most cases you can progress backwards into your ancestry through the initial periods without death certificates.

Once you have located your family's whereabouts with some degree of accuracy through registrations of birth and marriage – sufficiently anyway for you to be able to search out whole family groups through the various census records (see page 39) – you may then be in a better position to search for death certificates. If you can establish that an ancestor was alive in the census of 1861, but only his widow is listed in that of 1871, then you have a defined ten-year period within which you can expect to trace his death. If the name is a common one, let us say John Robertson, you are still likely to find several possibles, but as you will know his approximate year of birth (and hence age) from the census entries, you may well be able to recognise your particular man. If such a search at that time proves difficult in the General Register Office, you can again opt for the local one, where the choice of possibles will be fewer, always assuming he died at, or close to, his home.

Unless you specifically need a death certificate of a particular family member to help you proceed further back, I suggest you leave such a search until you have accumulated more information to a point where it is easier for you to pin down the search. After all, if you have completed your census searches with any degree of success, you will have been able to find your ancestors' likely dates and places of birth, without the need of a death certificate. You will better understand this when you read Chapter 3.

A death certificate, when you have traced it, will show the following information:

> Date and place of death (often including the address)
> Date of registration
> Name in full
> Age
> Sex
> Rank or profession
> Cause of death
> Signature, description and residence of informant

The informant will often be a relative, perhaps a son or daughter, and often one at whose house the person died. Beware of taking the quoted age for a fact. The age was usually given by the informant, who may have been mistaken. In the past many old people didn't have a birth certificate and might only have had their memory to rely on. Old people may become forgetful or exaggerate their age in either direction. Many speak of being in their 81st year, by which they mean they have passed 80 and are on the way to 81, but this is often mistakenly interpreted to mean they are already past 81. One year can make a considerable difference if searching for a common name. So ages quoted at death, from whatever sources (death certificates, tombstones, obituaries, family bibles) must always be regarded with suspicion.

With an infant (someone under 16) the name of the father or mother is usually stated on a death certificate. For a wife or widow the husband may appear on the certificate, and can thus inform you of a fact you did not already know. An elderly ancestor may have lived at the time of death with a relative who was formerly unknown to you, and this may lead you to trace the origins of that son or daughter, which could be especially useful if you have otherwise hit an impasse with your own line.

For many reasons a death certificate may assist you materially and can help complete your pedigree chart. It can also help you trace a will, and wills can mention numerous relatives as well as properties. So it is always best to try to fill in death details by tracing a certificate when the death occurred after 1837. However, if you can manage without it in the initial stages, do so, and come back to it later.

Note that after 1866 the registration indexes show the age at death; before that date, only the name and district.

CIVIL REGISTRATION SEARCHES – DO IT YOURSELF OR NOT?

How much of this preliminary research you are able to do yourself will largely be governed by your circumstances and where you live. If it is easy for you to get to the General Register Office in London, or you enjoy travelling and have time, there is no difficulty in doing it yourself. However, if you live a long way from London and have neither the time nor inclination for travelling, you may well prefer to employ an agent to get you through this early Civil Registration records stage. In my view it is at the point where this stage is over and your basic certificates of birth and marriage have been obtained, that the real quest begins, and takes on much greater interest. Then, you will almost certainly want to follow the trails yourself, unless you are a reluctant traveller, or prefer to remain an armchair genealogist (many people do this – quite successfully).

If you want to go ahead yourself it is possible to apply direct to the General Register Office by post and to ask the staff to undertake a search on your behalf, which they will do for a fee. However, the staff can only undertake a search limited to a five-year period. Therefore, if you have guessed the date of a birth incorrectly, such a search could fail to trace it, and you would need to follow up with a second request plus fee. If your initial information was woolly, you might need two or three attempts involving both delay and higher cost.

With any luck an agent can get you through Civil Registration research on one visit because he is familiar with the system and knows exactly where to look. A reason why an agent may probably be your best approach is that even if your postal application is successful first time and you find the required birth, you might want to continue to look for other births to the same couple to give you an accurate address for them at a date close to a census year (1841, 51, 61, etc.). If your original birth fell about midway between censuses there is a greater chance that they will not be traced at that address in the census(es). If the family lived at a different house in the same village, this might not be a problem. But if they were in a large city, or were highly mobile, then you might end up in a massive and futile search of a city census. These periods, of course were those when much of the population was on the move because of the draw of labour into town factories.

You can easily ask your agent to find a required birth, then move back or forwards to locate another birth to this couple as close as possible to a census year, then move back to locate the marriage of the parents, then on the birth of the groom (once again shuffling for a brother or sister close to a census year). Your agent may be able to achieve all this for you in the one session, and for a single fee, which gets you quickly and painlessly to the next stage of your quest.

MICROFILM OF NATIONAL INDEXES

In recent years copies of a microfilm of the national indexes have been made and these can be consulted in the central libraries of a dozen or so large towns in England and Wales. Not all go back as far as 1837, not all cover births, marriages and deaths (though many do) and few follow through more recently than 1912. These microfilm indexes can also be consulted at the local Family History Libraries of the Church of Jesus Christ of Latter-day Saints (the Mormons). There are now many of these throughout the United Kingdom and their facilities are open to all, regardless of religious belief. If one exists near you, you will find it a priceless asset.

Use of these indexes alone may not help you to recognise for certain a birth, marriage or death as the one you want, and details need to be confirmed from the records themselves. The indexes will be useful in showing the spread of the name in the area, or even throughout the country but you will still need to apply to the General Register Office for such checks and certificates.

The Society of Genealogists now has a microfiche copy of the birth indexes for England and Wales 1837–1901.

If you decide to use an agent, details of how to go about finding one are in Chapter 20, page 165.

3 CENSUS RECORDS

A population census has been held in England and Wales every ten years since the year 1801. There was no census in 1941, of course, because the country was at war. The original census returns are kept at the Public Record Office, Chancery Lane, London WC2A 1LR, where you or your agent may search them.

The Society of Genealogists also has copies of some census returns and indexes on microfilm.

In recent years, however, a large number of census returns from all over the country have been microfilmed and indexed by the Family History Unit of the Church of Jesus Christ of Latter-day Saints (the Mormons), who have placed the results of their amazing service at the disposal of any present-day genealogist. These are all to be found in Mormon libraries.

Copies of this microfilm are also available in other places and it will be well worth your while to search for one that is reasonably near you. Many County Record Offices have copies (for their own county if not perhaps for the whole country), so do the major public libraries.

Some local Family History Societies have undertaken the work of indexing census returns within their locality, and this work still continues. If you are lucky and find that your area of interest has been indexed, this is a wonderful short cut to locating your family, and you will also be able to extract other same-name families who might later prove to be related.

These facilities of locally-available census microfilms and indexes did not exist even a few years ago, so the present-day researcher has a tremendous advantage over those of the past. To find out what exists, and where you will find it, you should consult two booklets by J. S. W. Gibson, published by the Federation of Family History Societies, and revised regularly:

> *Census Returns 1841–1881 on Microfilm: A Directory of*
> *   Local Holdings* and
> *Marriage, Census and Other Indexes for Family Historians*

USE OF CENSUS DATA TO GENEALOGISTS

The genealogist may consult censuses over 100 years old. In certain circumstances permission may be given for officials to search the records of a census less than 100 years old, though these will seldom be needed for genealogical research. To obtain information from a census less than 100 years old and not yet open to public search you should write to the Registrar General at the General Register Office. You will have to provide a precise address, and you may be asked to declare that the information will not be used

City or Borough of *Chapelry*							
Parish or Township of *Burbage*						*Enumeration Schedule.*	

	HOUSES		NAMES	AGE and SEX		PROFESSION, TRADE, EMPLOYMENT, or of INDEPENDENT MEANS.	Where Born	
PLACE	Uninhabited or Building	Inhabited	of each Person who abode therein the preceding Night.	Males	Females		Whether Born in same County	Whether Born in Scotland, Ireland, or Foreign Parts.
Old Workhouse		1	John Dawson	35		Ag. Lab.	y	
			Elizabeth Do		30		y	
			John Do	10			y	
			Jane Smith		20		y	
		1	Barell Watts	45		Ag. Lab.	n	
			Mary Do		40		n	
			Sarah Do		15		y	
			William Do	10			y	
			Rachel Do		7		y	
			Thomas Do	5			y	
Burbage Cottage		1	William Loomes	30		Bricklayer	y	
			Mary Do		30		y	
			Emerlan Do		7		y	
			Robert Do	6			y	
			Sarah Do		4		y	
			Betsey Do		3		y	
			Susan Do		7 mos		y	
			Timothy Do	25			y	
			Edward Do	20			y	
			Elizabeth Do		13		y	
TOTAL in Page 6 }				9	11			

Fig. 3.1 *Extracts from the 1841 census showing questions and entries.*

in litigation.

For most genealogical research however you will be concerned with census records exceeding 100 years in age. The oldest census of potential interest is that of 1841, as earlier ones, from 1801–1831, record only statistics, not names. The dates when the census was taken varied year by year. These dates were:

1841	7 June
1851	30/31 March
1861	7/8 April
1871	2/3 April
1881	3/4 April
1891	5/6 April

The 1841 census might seem potentially the most helpful, being the oldest. However the information it called for was less detailed than that of the later censuses and, even though it might contain details of an ancestor who died before 1851, it is generally true that later censuses are more reliable as well as more detailed.

Before a search is attempted it is advisable to try to pin down as closely as possible the address of your family near to the census date. With a small village it is not usually too difficult a task to search through every household in the census returns until the right one is found. With a town or city, however, such a search could be very time-consuming and costly. A street address is almost essential, or at the very least a district address, when searching a large town. For places with over 40,000 inhabitants the census returns themselves usually have street indexes to help you locate the street you require.

An extract from the census of 1841

Fig. 3.1 shows entries from a page for the Chapelry of Burbage, Leicestershire:

Quite often several families or family groups shared a building, as they have here. The presence of a single oblique line (/) signifies the start of a particular household group within the building. The double oblique (//) denotes the end of the entry for that building.

The relationships of people within the household to each other is not stated. In the case of a man with wife and children this may well seem obvious, though it is all too easy to make false assumptions. In the case of William Loomes and his wife, Mary, their children end with Susan. Timothy and Edward were brothers of William living as a separate household within the same building with Elizabeth aged 13. Who Elizabeth was I do not know.

The trade or profession was normally given for those at work, that is, of working age. However this particular enumerator seems to have taken his instructions to mean the trade of the head of household only.

The Y indicates 'Yes' in answer to the question whether born in the same county. 'No' would be indicated by N. If born in Scotland then S was inserted, with I for Ireland and F for foreign parts. For censuses taken in Scotland or Ireland, E was inserted to indicate England or Wales.

Emerlan Loomes was in fact Emily, and probably the father pronounced this with a local accent as Emerluh, and the enumerator wrote down what he thought he heard. First names only were to be recorded, so that Sarah Jane might be recorded as Sarah or Jane, or perhaps some family form such as Sally or even Sal.

This was the first census where personal details were written down. No doubt families felt uneasy about official interference. Some perhaps felt they should give the 'correct' form of a name rather than the pet name. In this particular family the girl entered as Susan was normally Susannah, but whether the father gave the name differently or the enumerator felt that Susan was some more proper form, we shall never know.

The system of recording ages in this census needs explanation. Ages were given accurately for those aged 15 years or less, though an infant is often given in months. Ages over 15 were rounded *down* to the nearest five-year unit below. This means that 30 was recorded as 30, 31 also as 30, 34 also as 30, 35 as 35, and so on. On the form the age of 30 means 30 years old or more but not yet 35.

Because of possible embarrassment concerning the difference in ages of a married couple, by no means everyone told the truth to the enumerator. This was especially so in the census of 1841, and less likely to be so in later censuses because of this method of recording ages. A husband who was 34 would have been recorded in 1841 as 30, while his 35-year-old wife would have been set down as 35, giving an apparent considerable gap between them. It was not unusual for couples of disparate ages to 'adjust' them to a more convenient mid-point. It is not unknown even today for ladies to be sparing with the truth about their ages and some have been known to stick at 39 for years.

It is interesting that in the census return above, William Loomes, the oldest son, had all his younger brothers and sisters living in his house. In the same village however but living separately in someone else's house as a lodger was his mother, Elizabeth Loomes, a widow. In fact she was his step-mother, having married his father after the death of his first wife (the mother of all the children). Presumably the children did not get on with the step-mother, who was still alive, aged 80, in the 1851 census. The point of mentioning this is that one should not necessarily stop the search when the desired entry is found, as other family entries may also emerge which may be unexpected. So with a village or smaller town it may be as well to search it entirely and record all members of the surname.

The census entries listed only those people who stayed overnight in the house on the night of the census till the morning after, but it included nightworkers normally resident there. If a person happened to be away visiting relatives or on business or in a hotel, that person was included at the house in which he spent the night. This means that if a person you expected to find in the household is not recorded (such as the head of the household), his absence may be no more than that, not necessarily an indication that he had died. Conversely you may run into an unexpected and unknown visitor staying overnight with your family. Sometimes such a person may have been visiting in the course of business or may have been a distant and unrecognised relative. This is very likely the case with thirteen-year-old Elizabeth Loomes in the entry quoted – she may have been a distant niece or cousin, but I never did find out.

Certain abbreviations were commonly used for trades regularly met with in the district. 'Ag.Lab' means agricultural labourer, 'F.S.' means female servant, 'M.S.' male servant, 'F.W.K.' framework knitter, 'Stg.K.' stocking knitter. and 'Ind.' means of independent means. No doubt numerous abbreviations were coined in individual localities to suit local trades, and you will be able to guess at those you encounter.

The censuses of 1851 and later

From many points of view the censuses of 1851 and later are more helpful to a genealogist than that of 1841. This is principally because certain of the questions asked were more precise. Most important was age and place of birth. With later censuses however the initial shyness and resentment at intrusion into personal privacy had subsided somewhat, and the participants were less inclined to 'adjust' personal details or even to lie. Those who felt shame or embarrassment at a child born illegitimately or even incestuously would no doubt have covered up that fact by whatever means they could. The earlier parish registers might well have recorded the baptism of a child by including the vicar's own personal comments – a bastard child could well be so described, or perhaps as 'base begotten' or 'begotten in fornication with (the named party)'. By the time of the censuses, however, even the parish registers tended to record such events in a less scathing manner, though everyone in the village might know the scandalous details. Those giving details to the census enumerator may have accepted that their indiscretion was known locally, but may have felt very differently about broadcasting such details to a stranger at the door, writing it down for the 'government'. The point ultimately is that we cannot entirely rely on details in any census, but the later, more detailed ones tend to be less unreliable than the earlier ones.

The census of 1851 shows the same family at Windross End, in the chapelry of Burbage as shown in Fig. 3.2 on the next page.

In this instance young Emily is recorded as such and not as Emerlan. Occupations of all are given, including children at school.

Chapelry of Burbage

No. of Householder's Schedule	Name of Street, Place, or Road, and Name or No. of House	Name and Surname of each Person who abode in the house, on the Night of the 30th March, 1851	Relation to Head of Family	Condition	Age of Males	Age of Females	Rank, Profession, or Occupation	Where Born	Whether Blind, or Deaf-and-Dumb
72	Windsors End	William Loomes	Head	Mar	42		Bricklayer	Leicestersh. Burbage	
		Mary Do	Wife	Mar		43		Do ; Do	
		Emily Do	Daur			17		Do ; Do	
		Robert Do	Son		16		Bricklayer	Do ; Do	
		Betsey Do	Daur			13	Scholar	Do ; Do	
		Susannah Do	Daur			10	Do	Do ; Do	
		Frances Do	Daur			8	Do	Do ; Do	
		Martha Do	Daur			6	Do	Do ; Do	
		Thomas Do	Son		3			Do ; Do	
				Total of Persons ...	3	6			

I ——— U ——— B ———

Total of Houses

Fig. 3.2   *Extracts from the 1851 census showing questions and entries.*

Not all children stayed on at school and in the same census in this village is recorded a nine-year-old boy working as a cotton winder and a six-year-old girl working as a seamer of stockings, as well as other young children at work. So the fact that chidlren were scholars in itself tells something of the financial status of the family.

Those unmarried were often marked 'U', but sometimes this was just assumed. Married wives (i.e., not widows) might have their occupation panel left blank, as in the above entry, or might have it completed. Some were noted as 'wife', some given description, such as 'farmer's wife', 'whitesmith's wife', some were noted, for instance, as 'cotton winder'. It is difficult to know whether any real significance can be deduced from this as it may have been more a matter of the individual enumerator's method or whim than a sign that one wife did housekeeping only and another went out to work, or that yet a third helped her husband in his business.

Those in business and employing others might be styled, for instance, as 'clockmaker employing 2 men and 1 appr(entice)' or 'whitesmith, 5 men 3 app' (even if the employees did not live in the house). Relationship to the head of the household is not always specified, though commonplace ones usually were, such as aunt, niece, mother-in-law. A more complex relative might just be styled 'relative', perhaps for want of descriptive space. Some people did not know the answer to the questions and might give the place of birth as, say, 'Lancashire, NK.', meaning some place not known in Lancashire. Those who kept lodging houses had to include those there for the night of course. One such household in Kendal, Westmoreland, in the 1851 census included, in addition to the householder's own family, no less than ten lodgers, some evidently in transit – a 59-year-old labourer born in Cavan, Ireland, a 22-year-old 'traveller with pack' born in Ennis, Ireland, and two other young male travellers with pack born in Ripon, Yorkshire and Ulverstone, Lancashire. In the same census in the House of Correction was a 42-year-old 'prisoner' born Boston, USA.

It is always good policy to search *each* census of those open to the public, as these are amongst the most helpful and reliable of all the records you will use. You should note all entries of the required surname as some may later turn out to be related whom you do not recognise at first sight. When you have gathered together your census data and spent time sorting out the various family groups of interest, you will most likely then pass on to the next type of record, parish registers, but you may not have finished with census records for good. At some later stage, perhaps when you have uncovered another generation or two of your ancestry, you may wish to come back to census records to locate the families of a bride. It may be that they were living in the parish whose census you have already searched, but until you become aware of the bride's maiden name, this would not be apparent to you. The reasons for this will emerge more fully later, but basically it is because you might be looking for clues in the bride's family to help you overcome an obstacle in the male line. This secondary use of census records may not apply in your own family history, but can be a very useful aid in certain cases. It is sufficient at this stage to say that census returns can often be of more help in your research than that which is immediately obvious when you first consult them. This applies to other types of record too; you may well have to return to the same records to search for different information.

4 Boundaries Old and New – Maps

As you progress in your research you will find you need to consult maps, special maps which show the information you need. At first you may have used your motorist's atlas or some general map which will pinpoint the village or town where your family lived. It will soon become apparent, however, that this will not do. Apart from other considerations, the presence on a modern map of such features as motorways, modern bridges, railways (current or defunct) and modern boundaries will positively impede your task as these may disguise ancient routes of communication rather than help you to find them. The maps you need exist but you will require guidance as to which kinds of map will show the features appropriate to your specific task.

THE DIFFERENT KINDS OF MAPS

For instance you will need maps which show the boundaries of individual parishes, especially the ancient parishes as they were before about 1840, as that is the period you will have to use in searching parish registers. You will need other maps to show the jurisdiction areas of courts in which your ancestor's will may have been proven before you can attempt to search for any probate records. But probably before any of those special purpose maps you will want to see the geography of the area as it was at the period of your research. What did the area look like then? How would your ancestors have seen it? Which roads would they have used? Which markets would they have attended? Was there a bridge across the river then or did crossing over involve a round trip of twenty miles?

Time spent in pondering over maps is never wasted; it will stand you in good stead time and again in future research, and is an enjoyable part of the whole process of tracing your family tree. Researching your ancestors is not some kind of race or competition where the first past the post wins a prize. Your ancestry has lain undiscovered for hundreds of years. There is no hurry. The records you need will not disappear overnight. Those who rush through the process will not only miss vital clues and details as they blunder along, but they may miss the pleasure of the search itself.

Old printed maps

You can of course visit the area, although it may have changed beyond all recognition and then you are faced with the problem of trying to guess what those changes have been. What you need, preferably before you make your visit, is to see a map of the area as it was during the time you are researching.

43

Maps of the counties of England and Wales have been published since the end of the sixteenth century; Scottish and Irish counties a little later. These were printed maps, sold as information sheets for the use of travellers of the day in just the same way as a modern map you might buy from your bookshop. Some are rare and costly collectors' items today, and some are commonplace and can still be bought for a few pounds from antiquarian bookshops or specialist dealers in old maps. A current list of such dealers can be found in the *Guide to the Antique Shops of Britain*, published annually by the Antique Collectors' Club, Woodbridge, Suffolk. But of course you don't have to buy them. You can refer to these in any local central library or museum; or, in many instances, you can buy a modern reproduction map; or you may be able to have a library map photocopied.

If you cannot see the geographical surroundings themselves in the physical reality in which your ancestors saw them, you *can* see a map showing the area as it then was. You can see it as they themselves would have seen it on a map of that period, and that is a magical experience. Each road, each river and bridge, each village, each scattered farmstead can be seen just as they saw them. If they planned a journey, made a visit to church or to market, or moved to a neighbouring village, you can see which road they took, how long the journey was, how likely they were to have gone by this road or that. It is the next best thing to being there and will put you in touch mentally with the sort of thought processes which they themselves experienced. Would they have made the five-mile treck across the moors in the snow to church, or would they have attended the neighbouring church in winter, three miles closer?

By all means visit the locality itself, but preferably after you have spent an evening or two pondering over the terrain on a printed map of the period and, if you can, take a copy of the map with you when you visit. Just what maps are available is something you will need to discover. The easiest way to do that is to read a book about old printed maps – there are several available such as the classic *Maps and Mapmakers* by R. V. Tooley (see Bibliography, Appendix B). However, some useful possible maps are listed on page 47.

You will read about and see examples of the earliest county maps, made in the 1570s by Christopher Saxton; the Dutch-made maps published by Blaeu and Jansson, used during the Civil War; the first road maps ever published in the late seventeenth century by John Ogilby; the large format county maps of the middle eighteenth century published by Emanuel Bowen (these are by far the most detailed and best-suited for your purpose). The Ordnance Survey maps began at the start of the nineteenth century and went through many editions.

Modern large-scale maps

If you want to study a small locality in great detail then you can buy a modern edition of the Ordnance Survey map. These exist in the six-inch to the mile form and in the massive-scaled twenty-five-inch to the mile version. Both are useful once you get down to a location where your family were settled for some time and you may be able to pick out individual farmsteads and hamlets, but of course they will only show features still there at the time of the latest survey. Some of the older features may have disappeared, including even churches. (A former church close to my own home is now under the waters of a reservoir, so a modern map would fail to show that it ever existed.)

These maps in libraries

Your local library, museum or record office will have a list of the maps they hold of their locality. Sometimes, if you are lucky, they may have local manuscript maps. These are of several types.

Manuscript maps

Estate maps   There is the one-off manuscript map in the form of a survey, perhaps made for a local landowner of his estate, and each such would be different from the next but could well show such features as boundaries, hedges, fields, dwellings and perhaps each field marked with the name of the tenant or neighbouring owner.

Enclosure award maps   Another type is the enclosure award map, which could be of any age but most would date no earlier than the late 18th century, and these show how common land was broken up, but may perhaps show other features not immediately connected with the enclosure itself such as the layout of the village. It is largely a matter of chance what survives in the way of estate or enclosure maps.

Tithe maps   A third type of map is the tithe map, which will date from about 1836 or shortly after. Traditionally farmers had paid one-tenth (hence the word tithe, meaning a tenth part) of their produce towards maintaining the church and clergy. In 1836 this was rationalised to a fixed cash sum and special maps were drawn up to show landowners' houses, gardens, fields, etc. At the same time a list of owners and occupiers was made out with the tithe rents due, for those parishes which still had not moved to a cash payment system. In practice this means that not every parish was covered, but something like four out of every five were surveyed in this way. Three copies were made: one for the parish, one for the Bishop and one for the government's central records. Any parish copies still surviving today might be in the parish chest, but have more likely been surrendered to the local record office. The Bishop's copies will also in all probability be with the Record Office. The governmental copy is today in the Public Record Office.

Fig. 4.1 *Detail from a map of North Yorkshire in Emanuel Bowen's* Large English Atlas, *1750.*

The place to enquire today about tithe maps, enclosure maps or any other manuscript maps is the local record office. A photocopy of one such for your parish of interest could be both interesting and very helpful to you.

USEFUL PRINTED MAPS

Of the published maps of the past, one of the most useful is the series of county maps from the *Large English Atlas* by Emanuel Bowen published between about 1750 and 1760. These are on a scale of about four miles to an inch and show roads, churches, schools, post stages, road distances between towns, market towns with market days, as well as having small panels of text concerning local industry and produce. If your family lived by one of the major coach roads (and of course you will not know this until you look at a map showing the post roads) then the strip road maps by John Ogilby published in 1676 (and with later editions) are the most detailed of the period at a scale of one inch to the mile, although they show only the geography immediately adjacent to the roads. But they do show landmarks, gallows posts, windmills, duck ponds, distances, choices of route (ye best way or ye worste way) and all those things your ancestors themselves would have seen on a daily or occasional basis.

Large-scale local maps

In almost every English county there was often a mapmaker who made a particularly large scale map at some time during the second half of the eighteenth century. This would tend to be a one-off map of the particular county rather than one of a set of county maps. The local library or record office is bound to know of such a map.

A study of one or more contemporary maps achieves certain objectives. It gives you a basic knowledge of the names and disposition of the places nearest to where you have so far tracked your ancestors and these are places you need to memorise as they will crop up repeatedly during your later searches. The fact that you know the names will also help you in reading awkward scripts or awkward handwriting of whatever period. But it does more than that. Old maps will give you a feel of the period, an acquaintance with old spellings, an affinity with the place where your ancestors lived, at the time they lived there. When you visit the place you will already be tuned in to the century concerned, so that you will fail to notice the garage and petrol pumps, the gas board showroom, the building society offices, and you will have learned to see with a kind of tunnel vision only those things which might have been there at the time of your family.

As you progress with your research you will at times be stuck, perhaps on several different occasions. It is then that your affinity with the period and the locality will come in most useful. You need to think as your ancestors may have thought. If they came from some location other than this, where might they have come from

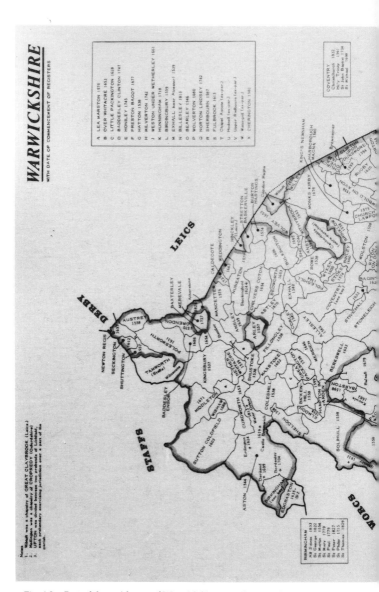

Fig. 4.2 *Part of the parish map of Warwickshire, one of a series from the* Atlas and Index of Parish Registers.

ECCLESIASTICAL JURISDICTIONS

Archdeaconry of Worcester
Archdeaconry of Coventry
Peculiars

Peculiar Jurisdictions

Royal Peculiar
Stratford

Peculiar of the Bishop of Lichfield
Avon Dassett, Shotteswell, Warmington

Peculiar of the Dean & Chapter of Lichfield
Arley, Edgbaston

Peculiar of the Chancellor of Worcester Cathedral
Wooburn Wawen

Peculiar of the Prebendary of Colwich
Bishop's Itchington

Peculiar of the Prebendary of Tachbrook
Bishop's Tachbrook

Peculiar of the Prebendaries of Ufton
Ufton

Peculiar of the Incumbent
Hampton Lucy

Budbrooke   Sherborne
Bubbenhall   Wolston
Knowle   Wroxhall   Packwood

SCALE [0 1 2 3 4 5 6 7 8 9 10] MILES

PUBLISHED BY THE INSTITUTE OF HERALDIC AND GENEALOGICAL STUDIES
NORTHGATE CANTERBURY ENGLAND   © 1963

and why? What would have drawn them to this particular village? What kind of trades did they follow and what openings might there have been in this place for such trades? You are at this stage going to have to try to guess where they may have come from before you can search the records of that parish, and the sooner you develop the knack, the easier it will be for you to pick up the trail again. There are little tricks of the trade which will help you pick up a lost trail, and we will come to those in due course.

PARISH REGISTER MAPS

Now we come to an altogether different kind of map, a kind you must have to enable you to know what records might exist, and in this the printed maps we have discussed so far are unlikely to help you, as even are manuscript maps of the locality. You need to know which church was a parish church in the past and what area that parish covered in the period before Civil Registration began (i.e., before 1837). There is no point in your hoping to search for your ancestors in the 1720s in the registers of a church which was not built till a hundred years later. Fortunately a series of maps has been compiled specifically for this purpose by dedicated researchers intended for people exactly like yourself. In some counties a local historical or antiquarian society or even a family history group may have compiled one. But one series of such maps has been compiled and published by the Institute of Heraldic and Genealogical Studies, Northgate, Canterbury, Kent CT1 1BA. These maps are available singly by county, or in a series as the *Atlas and Index of Parish Registers* edited by Cecil Humphery-Smith, FSA.

These maps show no geographical features other than the location of the parish churches and the boundaries of each parish territory, as well as the date at which the registers commence for each one. Some parishes contained in addition to the mother church, a chapel of ease, usually known as a chapelry. This was normally established at a later date than the parish church itself and its purpose was to ease the journey for more distant parishioners in a large-sized parish, as for instance, a moorland parish in North Yorkshire. The dates of commencement of the registers of a chapelry are also shown.

Large towns or cities such as London or York would contain very many churches and these maps will usually show the area covered by each.

Some parish maps appear in *Genealogical Research in England and Wales* (Volume 2) by David Gardner and Frank Smith, but these are on a smaller scale and are less clear.

MAPS OF PROBATE JURISDICTIONS

In addition to parish boundaries you will need to know the ecclesiastical jurisdictions before you can attempt to search for probate records. The series of maps published by the Institute of Heraldic and Genealogical Studies shows these areas too, as well as those parishes which were known as Peculiars, where special conditions pertained as far as records were concerned. In some counties local history societies have published their own genealogical maps, showing parish and other boundaries (such as ecclesiastical jurisdictions, Peculiars, etc.). The place to inquire about these is your local record office.

Modern Boundaries

One factor which is immediately obvious to most researchers is that of recent boundary changes whereby the present-day administrative districts will often no longer bear relationships to the original county boundaries. In a few instances the present-day boundary may be the same as that of the old county, but in most instances the modern district may consist of several parts of the original old counties. Naturally it is the old counties which are our principal concern, and it follows from the above that certain records of one old county may today be housed in a record office within part of a new district. This arrangement will vary between different County Record Offices or other repositories, and between different types of record, but whatever the arrangement it poses no problem as I shall explain later how you find out which office holds the particular type of record you require for your area of interest (see page 52).

What is not so obvious, however, is that with certain modern copies of records (microfilms, transcripts, etc.) a particular repository may have decided to stock copies of relevance to other nearby areas which *never at any time* came within its boundaries of jurisdiction, past or present, civil or ecclesiastical. The reason may be that some particular archivist or local research group may have wished to study an area linked by means of commercial, trade or geographical consideration, and these may not show up on any map. For example, certain Lancashire repositories stock microfilm copies of census returns for parts of Yorkshire that were never under Lancashire jurisdiction. So in studying your maps you will need to bear this in mind and note the presence of larger towns in adjacent counties to yours which are close to your area of interest – just in case.

5 RECORD OFFICES AND YOU

As soon as your more centralised initial searches are completed you are going to need to use the records in the local record office of the county where your family originated. We are speaking in terms of the old counties of course, and these have changed much both in name and territory with recent administrational boundary changes. The general principle with the old counties was that each had its County Record Office as a central repository for records. But even before modern boundary changes the position was far from straightforward, as some counties had more than one record office, and sometimes a record office within a particular county held documents relating to parts of other counties.

The documents you will want to use in your early stages of research are principally parish registers (and Bishop's Transcripts), probate documents and, perhaps, such things as marriage allegations (see page 72). In many cases all these documents will be kept within one record office.

Your principal task is to discover which office keeps the records of your area of interest, and you may have to do a certain amount of detective work to track it down. A record office may not necessarily hold records for its own immediate area, nor even an area close to its location. This situation arises not out of deliberate contrariness on the part of the administrative authorities, but because of changes in old boundaries, both ecclesiastical and civil, and is further aggravated by recent changes in administrative boundaries, some of which are likely to keep on changing.

As an example of what you might encounter – in Yorkshire there are three major record offices: at York, Leeds and Northallerton. Leeds was located within the old area known as the West Riding of Yorkshire, yet the records it holds concern the area which was formerly part of the North Riding, where Northallerton is located. To add to the confusion, many records for the old West Riding are actually at York!

WHERE ARE THE RECORD OFFICES?
A list of major record offices is set out in Appendix C, page 174. Additional ones can be looked up in the book *Repositories in Great Britain*, 8th edition (1987), published by the Royal Commission on Historical Manuscripts. You can buy a copy or consult one in any library. But unless you want to chart the record offices of the entire country you don't need such detailed documentation. You only want to establish which office holds the things you need.

THE WAY TO PROCEED
Most record offices have produced either a handlist or a small book

detailing the types of records they hold. These booklets also give advice on procedures for intending searchers. Once you think you have located the office you will want to use, your first step must be to write and ask for this booklet (for which there is usually a modest charge). You also need to know the office's opening hours and any special rules which pertain. This especially applies to the procedure for making appointments for research and whether it is necessary for you to obtain a reader's admission ticket.

If you locate your record office early in your researches, you can write to it immediately. Your centralised searches into Civil Registration records and Census Returns will take a week or two to complete, whether you do it in person or through an agent, so if, by the time this has happened, you already have full information from your record office, you know what parish registers, probate and other documents it holds, you will be able to move onwards with your searches without delay. In any event the handlist, or booklet, will stand you in good stead for many future searches, even if you decide to try using printed or manuscript copies of parish registers before turning to the originals.

The staff at record offices are generally very helpful provided you do not try their patience too far. If you explain in your initial letter the type of records you expect to want to use and the area of your interest then, if you happen to have selected the wrong record office, they will tell you which one you need. I suggest writing, not telephoning, as they can then consider your request under less harassed conditions, and you will be able to study their written reply at leisure, as a string of verbal responses may only confuse you at a time when you are barely familiar with the terms of reference.

The chances are that once you have pinpointed the county of origin of your ancestors before about 1820, you will find that they lived within that county for many generations before. People moved their homes much less before the coming of the railways and the attraction of workers to towns in the Industrial Revolution. Of course, you may find that your ancestors lived close to the boundary of an adjacent county, or even two adjacent ones, in which case your research may centre on parts of two or even more of the old counties. Generally speaking, however, you will be concentrating on your family origins within one 'home' county. If this is so, you may think you will be concerned only with one record office, and for many counties that will be true. But whether you need to deal with one or more repository depends on what records you wish to consult.

If your interest is in the holdings of original parish registers (and/or Bishop's Transcripts), then very often you will find that the major record office for the county has assembled together the majority of them under the one roof. If your interest is in probate records (wills, administrations, etc.) then you may find that these are more scattered. Probate records may be kept today in more than one record office within the county, or even, in certain cases, in a record office in some other county altogether – this depends very much on the old ecclesiastical boundaries.

SECONDARY RECORD REPOSITORIES AND OTHER SOURCES

Not all repositories are termed record offices. Some are departments of universities, or libraries or archives departments of a local council. But their function is the same – to preserve and make available for public use those documents within their care.

In some counties you will find that in addition to the major record office (or two) there will be other subsidiary ones, but even if you establish that the documents you require are kept in the major office(s), it is important not to ignore these secondary repositories. Some may house records pertinent to the town or city itself, for instance records of apprenticeship and freedom to trade, Quarter Sessions records, etc. It will probably be helpful to write to each repository within your 'home' county to establish just what they have, as the records held there may be useful to you at a later stage, and some of these may well be records you had not even thought about.

Bear in mind too that in addition to these large, subsidiary record offices and archives departments there may well be local libraries which may house certain kinds of records of interest to you, and these may be closer at hand or easier of access. Some local libraries may have copies of local census returns, the *International Genealogical Index* (IGI) for the immediate locality or county, newspapers or newspaper indexes, trades directories, obituaries, memorial inscriptions, parish register transcripts (manuscript or published). Find all this out as early as you can because there is no point in making arrangements with busy record offices to inspect some item which could well be available at a local library, where you might be able to walk in straight from the street.

We have already mentioned the Family History Societies and said that you should discover whether one exists in your area (step 5 of the sequence of search). You can find out by writing to the Federation of Family History Societies (see page 9), and if it does, join it.

Most important too is to find out where your nearest Mormon Family History Library is located. There are fifty-nine in Britain and although they are not actual record repositories, they do have (or can obtain) microfilm and microfiche of anything that has been copied (see page 178).

Don't forget the local Antiquarian Society, or Archaeological Society; they may well have collections or information relevant to your area of interest.

COUNTY RECORD OFFICES – WHAT THEY WILL AND WON'T DO FOR YOU

Record offices do not have the time or inclination to trace your family tree for you, but many of them would, out of courtesy, be willing to check on perhaps a single item from their holdings. If, for instance, you found that your ancestor Elijah Merryweather died in Bodmin in 1744, they mght just be willing to check whether they had any probate documents for him by looking at their calendars for 1744/5/6, and, if found, they would quote you a price for photocopies. Such a small search might be done free of charge, though don't bank on it, and if you try to make a habit of it, they will soon get wise to you. Most CROs do have a duplicated list of local record searchers, which they will send you for the price of a stamp, after which it is up to you to make your own arrangements for such a person to search on your behalf and to agree terms – that is, of course, if you can't, or don't want to go yourself.

On the other hand, some CROs today are willing to undertake searches on your behalf and they have a prescribed scale of charges for doing this on a commercial basis. Some also have published small booklets on how to use their records for genealogical purposes, and, if such a booklet is available, you would be wise to buy it as a guide through the vast maze of records they may hold. When you write to your local CRO, however, do not include a ten-page history of your family or detailed pedigrees, as staff have no time for all that. Keep your letter brief and to the point.

When you visit a CRO, do not turn the day into a trip for your wife, children, picnic hamper, flask and dog, as you will probably have to leave all of them in the car or the park, as CROs do not have facilities to cope. In many CROs you are not permitted even to take a briefcase in with you. You should therefore be equipped with pencils and a notebook, and assume that you can take nothing else in with you.

Many CROs will today expect you to search microfilm or microfiche copies rather than the originals. Do not be put off by this, as the readers are easy to use and if you have never used one before, the staff will set the machine up, and show you how to use it.

In the list of County Record Offices in Appendix C (page 174) the principal for most, though not all, of the old counties is that the CRO acts as a central repository and will be likely to house probate records, parish registers, Bishops' Transcripts and marriage licences as well as other records. Many of these were formerly in the diocesan record offices and have now been housed in the CRO for convenience, so that the CRO acts as a diocesan office for older documents.

6   PARISH REGISTERS AND WHERE TO FIND THEM

By the time you have completed your search through Civil
Registrations and the census records you will already have a sketch
of a pedigree taking shape. But you will still have only a part
picture of the period you have already covered. In particular you
may be lacking death dates for some individuals, even your direct
ancestors, as well as great aunts and uncles. You may never find
out what became of some of the sidelines, but stray details may fit
in later, as you progress, like pieces in a jigsaw puzzle. At this
stage, however, it is probably inadvisable to make specific searches
for these details. With a little luck a few will emerge anyway as
you search for other things.

If your census searches have been even moderately successful
you may well now have your first ancestor's birth period in the
late 18th century, or perhaps the early nineteenth. The temptation
is now to jump back to look for the baptism of your oldest named
ancestor, perhaps, say, in Northallerton in 1797, as the census
leads you to believe. Before you do, consider first one or two facts
about parish registers, which we have mentioned frequently, but
not discussed in detail.

WHAT ARE PARISH REGISTERS?

The parish registers were the books in which the vicar of the local
Anglican church, or another person acting at his request, would
list all those events concerning his parishioners, most notably
details of baptisms, marriages and burials. Such registers were first
ordered to be kept in 1538. Few today go back as far as that, partly
because the law was not always complied with at first and partly
because, over the centuries, some old register books have been
lost. At this stage you are not particularly concerned with how far
back registers may go because you are hoping to find such
information as you want from the much more modern periods (late
18th or early 19th centuries) when they almost certainly *will* be
preserved. Much later in the search you may wish to know about
the earliest registers for your particular parish, and we will come
to that problem later.

Just what form the registers take will depend partly on the size
of the town or village and partly on the period in question. Small
country churches might have baptised no more than two or three
children in a year; large towns would have hundreds, even
thousands of baptisms a year. Where in the judgement of the vicar
of the day, or perhaps the parish clerk, these entries would not be
very numerous, it may well be that baptisms, marriages and
burials would appear in the same volume in the order they
occurred rather than in separate volumes each under a specific

category of event. So for a small village a single volume might contain all entries of whatever type, and not necessarily in annual order, but perhaps in a mixed-up jumble. Such a register may have no clear headings, and burials might be jotted occasionally amongst the baptisms. It is not uncommon, when searching an early register of what you took to be baptisms, to see an occasional age given: John Roberts aged 32; Mary Hardacre aged 70. Eventually you realise the clerk has begun to record burials in what was intended to be the baptisms listings, though you have always to be on the alert because people were sometimes baptised as adults.

After 1754 a separate register had to be kept for marriages, as required under Lord Hardwicke's Marriage Act, though baptisms and burials might still appear in a joint volume. After 1812, Rose's Act required that a separate register be kept for marriages, baptisms and burials. It is therefore likely that when your search begins, each event you head will be in a register of the appropriate category. Parish registers are still kept in this form to the present day.

WHAT IS A PARISH?

Before you can begin your own searches into parish registers you need to know whether the place of birth given in the census records was in fact a parish, that is, a village with a church. If it was not, then under which parish would it have fallen?

To complicate things further you may well have found a family group in the census showing different places of birth for several of the children meaning that they might have moved from village to village with a change of employment. So you may need to check the registers of several parishes to confirm the facts, also to identify any additional children who may have been born there and died young or between censuses. Perhaps too you might come across the burial of a grandparent or some other elderly relative of whose existence you were previously unaware. It is important that when you do begin to search the registers you should note every entry for that surname as some may well turn out to be relatives. Even variant spellings should be recorded too.

You may need to search a multi-volume gazeteer of the mid-19th century. Lewis's *Topographical Dictionary* is a favourite, though personally I use Fullarton's *Parliamentary Gazeteer*. Such a work will tell you the location of the place, whether it was a parish and, if not, under which parish it came. It also tells such things as population number, number of houses, number of schools and so on. The chances are you will have already located the county from the census, so if there are several places with the same name you will easily identify the one you want.

A little care is required in establishing what exactly a parish was because there were two kinds. The first, with which you are concerned, is an ecclesiastical parish, the area covered by a church and its registers. The population living within its boundaries were required to attend its church – by law, by custom or by inclination –

these varying at different periods. An ecclesiastical parish contained at least one church, usually known as the parish church (sometimes the mother church), or it might also contain a number of smaller churches, known as chapelries or chapels of ease. Chapelries were usually established at a later date than the parish church itself, generally to cope with the larger population or for convenience of those living far away in a large parish.

The second kind of parish is the civil parish, that is, an administrative area which might or might not conform in its boundaries to an ecclesiastical parish.

In your research, the questions to which you will need answers are:

★ which ecclesiastical parish covered the place where your ancestors lived *at that period*?

★ did the parish contain one or more chapelries?

★ do the registers of each survive and for what periods?

★ if the chapelry registers began at a date later than those of the mother parish church, what was that date?

This may sound a very complex business, but once you have found the county of your ancestor's birthplace, the rest has been done for you and is very conveniently set out on one of the special parish register maps described on page 50.

Let us take an example and imagine you are hoping to find your ancestors in a place called Hartwith in Yorkshire. From Fullarton you would learn that Hartwith, correctly named Hartwith with Winsley, was a chapelry within the parish of Kirkby Malzeard in the West Riding of Yorkshire. Today it lies in the North Riding due to modern changes in boundaries, but of course you need to relate to pre-1840 boundaries. From a parish register map you would see that Hartwith registers begin in 1751, those of Kirkby Malzeard in 1653. For periods before 1751 therefore you would expect to find your family documented in the registers of the mother church not the chapelry.

In fact Hartwith is one of those odd chapelries, its territory lying some distance from Kirkby Malzeard from which it is separated by the territories of two other parishes, Ripon and Pateley Bridge. A visit to the mother church from Hartwith involved about six miles of travel each way. In winter weather it is unlikely a family would trudge with young children across snow-covered moors. Instead they may well have attended a closer church, of which they had a choice of four, even though none of these was strictly speaking their own parish church. Such a separate chapelry, which is some distance apart from the mother church, is known as a detached parish. Most chapelries will be found to lie within the overall boundary of the parish itself, as is the case with the other chapelry of Kirkby Malzeard parish, named Middlesmoor, where registers begin from 1700.

In reality a search for ancestors in a parish with chapelries might involve a search not only of the registers of the mother church but of each chapelry too, and quite likely the registers of each adjacent parish. Your ancestors, even if living as a family in Hartwith, might have decided to attend Middlesmoor church so that they could have Sunday lunch with the in-laws.

Each church or chapelry may have drawn in parishioners in a different way at different periods. Often it will be found that a family might use the local chapelry for baptisms (sometimes written down under 'christenings', which means the same thing) and perhaps for burials too. But for a wedding they may well have opted to use the mother church, perhaps because it was a more imposing building, or it might all the more impress the neighbours. For reasons we may never know, the registers of chapelries often contain no marriages, those being recorded instead in the registers of the mother church. On the other hand it is always dangerous to make assumptions, and the careful researcher would check both.

WHERE TO FIND PARISH REGISTER RECORDS

Suppose you have located the parish, learned when its registers begin, and are now anxious to start the most exciting part – that of searching out the actual events of your ancestors' lives from the parish registers.

You might think of getting into the car and having a run over to the church, hoping to catch the vicar in a receptive mood. Don't! Do not even adopt the more courteous approach of writing to ask him for an appointment to call and search his registers, or even if he might be willing to search on your behalf. It would be wasting his time and yours because very few parish registers now reside in the church safe.

By far the majority of the originals (except for the present-day ones of course) have been handed over for safe keeping to the local County Record Office (CRO) or Archives Department. When you are ready to search, this is where you will have to apply, and today you may well have to make an appointment beforehand because demand for access usually exceeds seating space.

As yet however you are not ready to search the original registers as there are other avenues it may be best for you to approach first. You need to know in what form the parish registers exist. The vicar's method of writing up registers would doubtless have varied from parish to parish. Did he do them on one evening a week? Once every month or two? Evidence suggests that it was for the most part an infrequent task, perhaps put off as long as possible. Prior to writing up his registers in the neatest possible form, evidence also suggests that the names of the various parties were jotted down on slips of paper some of which got lost, thus accounting for the occasional missing ancestral entry.

Bishop's Transcripts

One reason we know about lost entries is because from 1579 a duplicate copy of the parish registers had to be made and submitted annually to the Bishop's custody. These duplicate registers were normally on loose sheets of parchment, several sheets for larger parishes, and known as the 'Bishop's Transcripts'. Most parishes complied with the requirement of submitting an annual duplicate copy, though after 1813 the practice was not always continued in every parish. For the most part the Bishop's Transcripts are well preserved and form a very useful means of cross-checking with the original registers. Sometimes items will appear in one and not appear in the other. Sometimes entries were abbreviated in one, yet written in full in the other. Where an original register has been lost, the Bishop's Trancripts form a vital alternative copy. Until recent years the BTs (as they are often known) were usually kept in the Diocesan Registry, but many are today housed in the local record office, where the original registers are also kept.

Published forms of Parish Registers

Sometimes a parish register may have been copied out in full and pehaps indexed too. Some are manuscript copies, some are type-script, some have even been published by local history societies. A search in a published volume of parish registers, all of which are normally indexed too, is obviously very much easier and quicker than a search in the originals – even though any published or transcribed version is likely to contain occasional errors. There is little point in travelling the length of Britain to search in the original registers of a particular parish, if a published volume could be consulted in your local library, or even borrowed and studied at home through a library such as that of the Society of Genealogists.

Before you begin searching it is always essential to investigate where the most conveniently-located records can be found, or the most convenient form of them. The Society of Genealogists publish a small volume listing all those parish register copies held in their library (many, though not all, can be borrowed by members). The Society also publishes another small book listing all those register copies whose whereabouts are known but are *not* in their library. A more detailed multi-volume work has already been published by them covering certain counties only, known as the *National Index of Parish Registers*, and this is extremely helpful provided it includes the county you need. This publication also lists the whereabouts of the original parish registers and the Bishop's Transcripts for those counties. Ultimately the series will cover the whole country, but completion is still some years away.

The *Phillimore Atlas and Index of Parish Registers*, edited by C. R. Humphery-Smith and published by Phillimore, shows on each county map the individual parishes, being an atlas consisting of those parish register maps we mentioned earlier (see page 50). It also shows what registers survive, where deposited, what registers have been copied and what parishes are included in the *International Genealogical Index* (see page 62) as at publication date (1984).

Any local County Record Office will almost certainly have a duplicated listing of those parishes whose original registers they hold, those whose Bishop's Transcripts they hold (or their whereabouts if elsewhere) and quite probably also of any published volumes or manuscript, or typescript copies, of parish registers within their sphere of interest. Sooner or later you will need to contact them anyway to look at the originals, but initially you can establish by postal enquiry just what they hold and for what periods. They will probably make a small charge to cover postage costs in mailing such a leaflet.

The whereabouts of Bishops' Transcripts can be established by consulting Jeremy Gibson's booklet *Bishops' Transcripts and Marriage Licences, Bonds and Allegations* published by the Federation of Family History Societies (1991) and this also lists the whereabouts of microfilm copies. In most counties the BTs will be housed in the same record office as the original registers of the same parish.

Many counties will have a local history society or local antiquarian society, some of whom themselves publish copies of local parish registers as well as many other interesting local records, which you may wish to consult later. At the initial stages of your research you would be well advised to write and ask them for a listing of holdings of parish register transcripts.

Most published and many transcribed copies of parish registers will cover the period only up to 1812, after which you will need to consult the originals or BTs. The reason for this is that the better quality of originals post-1812 are in any event easy to read and usually well preserved, and the urgency of publishing or transcribing was to preserve those registers of greatest age and most liable to deterioration. Some have been copied only for their very oldest periods and might end in the mid-17th century. Some might be marriages only, and most important of all is that you must watch for some copies which are excerpts only. Modern practice tends to be to copy registers in their entirety and to run up to 1837, but some older publications copied selected entries only. If you mistakenly search a volume of extracts you might be led into believing your family were not from that parish, so in general there is little point in using a copy unless it is a complete transcript. Perhaps even more dangerous are the few transcripts which have been abbreviated to keep the publishing cost down. Some of these may list names only and omit vital details such as profession, abode or age, which could be found in the originals. Always therefore check very carefully in the introduction as to just what method of transcribing has been used, and check too for any missing years.

Most registers will have a year or two missing here and there, or even whole pockets of several years. Modern publications usually try to fill these gaps by transcribing the BTs for such periods, but sometimes the BTs too are defective for the years in question.

Any copies will contain errors. Even with the highest skills at reading old scripts and with the utmost care taken to transcribe, slips will appear in the printed form. Often the copyist mis-reads a flourishing initial letter, and will naturally also mis-index it. This is most likely with uncommon names. I have found examples of my own name mis-transcribed as Toomes, Goomes, Zoomes, Townes, Lownes and almost any imaginable combination of initial letter. The experienced searcher will skip through the index for any, often isolated, examples of mis-indexing – anything which looks a little like the required name and especially if only a single instance of it appears.

Furthermore the cautious researcher will not only search out those entries he wants from the index, but he will search the registers line by line in case any single entry for his ancestors has been missed in the index. It is a very easy job in a published or typescript copy. Failure to do so may mean missing an important fact for ever.

Having found at least some of the required facts from a register transcript, the wise researcher should then also check at least the most important entries in the original parish registers *and* in the BTs. It is by no means uncommon for information to appear in one which is not in the other. To make haste by omitting any such search, even though it might seem boringly duplicate, is to risk missing vital leads. Even such minor details as the names of witnesses may well contain helpful clues – quite often the names of witnesses to a marriage for instance may have been omitted in a published copy.

The International Genealogical Index (IGI)

There is yet another important type of record of which you should be aware: this is known as the *International Genealogical Index* (the IGI), formerly called the *Computer File Index*, the latter title now fallen out of use. It is a massive index in microfilche and was compiled (and is still being expanded) by the Genealogical Society of Utah for the Church of Jesus Christ of Latter Day Saints (the Mormons). It contains over fifty million baptisms as well as some marriages and burials. Each entry is indexed under surname for each county, and some counties are covered in greater completeness than others, though no county is covered for every parish. A great many of the items in the IGI are from parish registers which were published in the past. This means that any errors in the published registers are transcribed into the IGI too, and of course in any transcribing task of this immense magnitude more errors will have crept in along the way.

The IGI is strongest in its coverage of baptisms, far less strong on marriages, and weakest on burials. The presence of some items from a particular parish register is no proof that *all* items from it will appear. In other words if you find the baptism of any ancestors in the IGI from a certain parish it is quite possible that there might be a ancestral marriages and/or burials there too, even though these might not show up in the IGI.

Many county record offices now have a copy of their own county's section of the IGI, and so do some larger libraries. This means that in any region there is often more than one copy of the IGI available. You will need to find just where they are sited in each county or region by consulting *Where to find the International Genealogical Index* by Jeremy Gibson and Michael Walcot, published by the Federation of Family History Societies. This will advise you of the numerous places where you can find a copy of the index for your region of interest. Some, but by no means all, of these libraries offer a printout service and the first printout sheet you should obtain is that (found at the front of each county section) indicating what parishes are covered within the county. Without this you will not know if the absence of your required names arises because none appear in that parish, or because the parish itself is not covered or, worse, if only *part* of the parish register is entered and you have assumed that all its registers are included.

The IGI is constantly expanding and so great is its coverage now that few can resist turning to it for use as a sort of radar scanner of surnames for the area of interest. Today some researchers prefer to use the IGI even before searching census returns. The choice is yours.

Unless you have an extraordinarily unusual surname I would suggest that the census be used before even considering the IGI. Even a name you think is unusual will prove to be far less uncommon than you thought, and the chances are that an IGI search too early in your research will produce a whole heap of entries for the surname. This can prove bewildering, especially if you are new to genealogy, and can leave you in a spin, having picked up numerous possible ancestors in all kinds of random places. The census will lead you gently back one step at a time, with ancestors you *know* are yours.

Once you have passed the census stage, and ideally the first parish register search stage too, then a great many of the entries offered from the IGI are instantly and obviously eliminated and can cause you no confusion, though of course some of them may come in useful later on as perhaps being cousins or other kin of your ancestor. By the time you reach the IGI you will also be more experienced in handling parish register data and you will not be intimidated or misled by the sheer volume of entries offered.

Any vital entries found through the IGI should certainly be checked against the original registers, as very often additional information will be given there, and of course errors will be found by this means too. Personally I would also check the entries (the vital ones anyway) in the BTs, which again can sometimes give information which is not in the original registers. The most useful aspect of the IGI is that it will point you in the right direction, and especially to other nearby parishes where members of your surname and, perhaps, family lived at such time as your entries run out in your original parishes of search. It is not a substitute for searching the originals or BTs, and if you try using it in this way you will almost certainly miss vital additional facts, or draw up incorrect pedigrees through errors, or both.

USES OF THE PARISH REGISTER MAP

By this time you should have bought your own copy of a parish register map for the county of your interest, or of course the whole atlas of them, mentioned above. My suggestion is that you make full use of this in the way in which I used mine as a professional, working from two copies of each. One I would mark out by colour coding to show the location of original registers and BTs, using different colours. On another I would mark those parishes whose registers were published, those whose registers were transcribed, those in the IGI, and so on. You should do this for the parish of your immediate interest and for those which lie closest to it in every direction. This way you can see at a glance where you have access to the whole district with your main parish as its centre.

You will more than likely have to search the registers of each of these parishes in due course, even if your family lived only in one parish as far back as records go – which is most unlikely anyway. You will in any event probably want to tie up loose ends of family members who married in the next parish, brothers who moved there, and so on. The colour coding means that when searching the printed registers of one parish at a certain library, you can very quickly see which others are most useful for you to look at on that same visit. Forward planning is always essential. It can be a most enjoyable part of the research anyway, but it will ensure that your time in a record repository is used to best advantage when your visits and the number of hours available to you will always be limited.

WHAT IS IN THE PARISH REGISTERS?

Having first found out what exists and where you can gain access to it, what can you expect to find in a parish register? Well, the listings of baptisms (christenings), marriages and burials will be straightforward enough and there should be no problem with understanding the writing until back to the early 18th century, if then. Births rather than baptisms were recorded during the Commonwealth period (1653–1660) but entries relating to births without baptism date *at other periods* may well be indications of Nonconformity (see page 80).

The Commonwealth period can be a difficult one in parish registers because at that time the entries were to be kept as registrations of birth (not baptism), marriage and death by some local official, not the parish minister. The result is that in some parishes the records were well kept in this period, but in others they do not exist today at all (whether because they were never recorded or have been lost since is immaterial). In a good number of parishes, especially rural ones, life carried on much as usual despite the war, and some rural registers run through this period in perfect order. To some extent it is pot luck as to just what you find in this period, and all you can do is hope that you are not faced with seeking the birth (or baptism) of an ancestor in this very period in a parish without registers at that time. If things do work out like this for you, there are probably ways round the problem, so do not despair. Indeed with almost all the problems, there is usually a way round, but the detour will usually prove more costly and troublesome to pursue. There is a book written especially to help with such situations and described as 'a manual for analysing and solving genealogical problems in England and Wales, 1538 to the present day'. This is *The Family Tree Detective* by Colin D. Rogers, published by Manchester University Press, revised 1989.

A baptismal entry may sometimes state no more than the child's name, without parentage, but this is unusual except in the 16th century. Normally the father's name is given, often with the first name but not usually the maiden name of his wife. Just occasionally as at Skipton, Yorkshire, a clerk might have been extra careful. Here is a sample entry:

> Baptised Aug. 10 Catharine 3rd d. of William Chamberlain of Skipton, Timber Merchant, son of Abraham Chamberlain of Skipton, Timber Merchant, & Catherine d. of John Wilkinson late of Skipton, Plumber & Glazier (born 21st June).

Where a clerk did record an abnormally large amount of detail, he would often do this throughout his period of office, and such occasions, though rare, are a great genealogical boon.

Marriages will often record no more than the names of the two parties, but may well stipulate whether by licence or by banns, and after 1754 it will almost always specify. You should always note the method, as it may be possible to investigate further into banns or licences (see page 70).

In the period between 1783 and 1794 occasional baptism or burial entries may have the word 'pauper' alongside. At this period a tax was payable on registered entries and people denoted as paupers were excused. It is often thought that many entered as such were not really paupers but just wanted to avoid the tax.

Between 1666 and 1678 Acts were passed to ensure that all corpses were buried in woollen shrouds (to aid the wool trade), and many burial entries after that time may have the words 'in wool' or 'in woollen' after them. Sometimes instead the word 'affidavit' or 'affdt' appears, indicating that the vicar had received an affidavit to that fact, and occasional affidavits are written out in another book or on loose sheets. The practice slowly fell from use though the law was not repealed till 1814.

In searching for baptisms it must be borne in mind that the expectant young wife may well have gone back to her parents' home to have her first child (or even first few children) and the child may well have been baptised in that parish, which may not be the parish she normally lived in. This practice may have also been induced by the laws relating to settlement (see page 126). It is not therefore uncommon to find the first child or two baptised in a different parish from later children of a marriage. When, as sometimes happened, the bride was married from her parents' home in their local parish, *and* the first two children were baptised in that church, this can give a false impression of the couple having lived there for the first few years of married life.

There was no set period between birth and baptism, and sometimes a sickly child would be baptised at birth for fear it would not live long enough to achieve baptism in church. Sometimes burial entries appear for children who were not baptised, often when they died very young, and so a burial entry is not always balanced by a corresponding baptism.

Occasionally a family would baptise several children of varying ages at once, the ages ranging from a few weeks to the teens. This is not uncommon with lax churchgoers, and can happen especially when they move village and cannot remember which children have been baptised and which have not. The minister of the new parish might have insisted on doing them all for safety's sake, and this can be very puzzling when you find two or three children, whose baptisms you have already traced in one parish, being baptised again in a new one.

The failure to trace an occasional marriage or two can leave the researcher with a missing link problem. There can be all kinds of reasons, the most obvious being that the couple 'ran away' to get married in some distant place to escape parental displeasure, even though they were of full age. Some of these may fall into the category known as 'clandestine' marriages, which we will examine on page 79.

For a list of abbreviations and unfamiliar terms sometimes encountered in parish registers see page 90.

Double dating – Julian and Gregorian calendars post-1752

You will not have been searching long in parish registers before you come across double dating, for instance:

> Baptised 13th February 1692/3 Julian son of
> Archibald Smithers and Melissa his wife.

Until 1752 the first day of the year was 25 March and the last day, 24 March. The present-day system of beginning the year on 1 January 1752. The old calendar was the Julian calendar and the new system was known as the Gregorian calendar after Pope

Gregory XII, who introduced it in 1582, after which date most European countries used the new system. Britain did not change to the Gregorian calendar at that time because a system devised by a Catholic Pope was not acceptable, but eventually it was adopted in 1752.

Errors cumulating in the Julian calendar meant that by 1752 Britain was adrift by eleven days and so eleven days were omitted in September of the year 1752. Genealogists tend to use double dating from 1 January to 24 March inclusive in years before 1752 so that no confusion can arise as to which year is intended. The two systems are called Old Style and New Style.

The implications for genealogists are important. For example the month of February 1692 followed after July 1692. Suppose that Robert the son of William and Mary Arkwright was baptised in July 1692 and buried in February 1692, this might at first sight seem to relate to a quite different child. The child baptised in July could perhaps be mistaken for a *second* child of the same name replacing the first Robert who had been buried in February. By writing those dates between 1 January and 24 March with double dates in those years before 1752 (e.g., 18 February 1692/3) we avoid confusion. By such a double date we indicate the year *then* known as 1692 but *now* known as 1693.

When searching parish registers in particular it is important to watch out which dating system is being used, as some parishes were already using the New Style system *before* 1752. Even worse, a particular parish might use one system under one clerk, then switch to another under a different one, until finally ending up with the New Style system after 1752. Always be on your guard therefore when searching any records before 1752 in the months of January, February and March as dates will be written either using the Old Style or Old Style/New Style (for instance, 15 Jan 1727, or 15 Jan 1727/8). It is most unlikely that New Style will be used alone till after 1752 in original documents such as parish registers, but it might well be used in transcribed or published versions. To ensure which year is meant, always scan on to 25 March to see which new year is recorded since a slip in recording the correct year can throw you off the trail.

With Quaker records of any kind you should know that, while they used the same year system as everyone else, they did not use the same months, as they refused to call months (or days) by names based on heathen Gods. They called the days of the week by number, the First Day being Sunday. They also called the months by number, one to twelve, with the first month (before 1752) being March. Thus the date '1st 2nd 1692' would be 1 April 1692 (not, as might easily be mistaken, 1 Feb 1692/3. March, being a split month, might refer to the old or new year, and Quakers would often denote Old and New Style together for clarity. But watch out for switched dating 8/12/1720 might mean 8th day 12th month *or* 8th month 12th day!

In a legal document such as a will Quakers might write of 'the second month commonly called April' so that all knew what was meant while still indicating that they themselves did not use the name. A date engraved on an item might appear as 5 4 42, which looks like a number at first sight but would indicate 5th day 4th month 1742. I have seen such dates engraved on Quaker clocks and easily mistaken them for some sort of serial number.

7 MARRIAGES – BANNS, LICENCES, BONDS, INDEXES AND RUNAWAYS

Tracing a marriage can sometimes be difficult, or at least can mean scouting around a little further afield than for a baptism. It is not uncommon to find a family settled in a village with regular baptisms of what may appear to be the whole group of offspring, yet find that the couple were not married there. Of course I am speaking now of the period before Civil Registration began in 1837. A common reason for this might be that the groom worked in the parish where the married couple were to reside and where they baptised their subsequent children, but the marriage may have taken place in the *bride's* parish for reasons of family convenience – a custom still sometimes practised today.

In many cases the bride herself may have come from a neighbouring parish not too far distant, but a girl who worked as a household servant, for instance, may have met her groom many miles from her family home. It is important always to try to trace the marriage, even if, as sometimes happens, the groom's ancestry appears to run back in the village they later lived in, as you might deduce from baptismal entries from the right sort of period. Not only does the marriage itself make your pedigree more complete, but the marriage entry might well give additional information about the groom – age, occupation, sometimes even his parentage. While record of parentage is uncommon before 1837, there are some parishes where it was often recorded even into the eighteenth century. Additional details from the marriage may even be vital in order to establish which baptism of two or three possibles would fit your male ancestor.

The information in a parish register concerning a marriage may be scant. Occasionally it may not even list the bride's name. An entry such as: 'Married 15th July 1593 John Williams' is uncommon and this male-name-only type of entry is almost always confined to a few years in the late 16th and early 17th century in certain parishes only. For very many marriages, especially those before 1812, the entry may say no more than: 'Married 18th June 1775, George Williams and Mary Townley'. Once you find the marriage, or at least a marriage which looks as if it might be the one you want (for you may well come across several possibles requiring elimination) there are various methods by which you might find more detail than the bare facts in the register.

First, however, you have to locate a possible marriage, and there may be a few tricks of the trade which would help you. You will already know from your parish register map the names and existence of registers in those parishes closest to the one you have already tried. You will ideally work round, parish by parish, in an ever widening circle, but to do this in original parish registers may be slow and laborious and may mean several visits to a record office. It is here that a knowledge of published register transcripts will help, as these may be quickly searched, especially if, as usually is the case, they have been indexed. Many parish registers have been published for marriage entries only, and they are ideal for this purpose. Other registers may have been copied in typescript or manuscript or microfilm, and these too may be much simpler to search than the originals. The IGI is a marvellous tool for locating marriages, though obviously incomplete.

If, as I suggested earlier, you have marked up your parish register map in a colour-coded manner, you will be able to see at a glance which parish registers exist in transcribed form, or perhaps are included in the IGI (see page 62), for it is on occasions like this that the IGI may come into its own as a scanner index. Once you locate what appears to be the required marriage in one of these sources, it is then important for you to check the original entry in the register itself and, ideally, in the BTs too, because modern transcripts may often have abbreviated the marriage entry to names only. This may particularly be the case if you use one of the marriage indexes made on a county (or part-county) basis, as many of these were made as a quick location instrument rather than a detailed copy. However, before you turn to the registers themselves, it may assist you considerably to know how the marriage procedure worked in the past.

MARRIAGE PROCEDURES OF THE PAST

There were two basic ways in which a couple might marry, or plan to marry: one was by means of banns, the other by licence. For most of the historical periods with which we are concerned this marriage ceremony had to be performed in a church (or chapelry) of the establishment (the Church of England). Even if your ancestors were nonconformists, this applied. It also applied even if they went through a form of marriage in a nonconformist place of worship. Indeed, for most of the historical period concerned the marriage was not considered safely legal unless a Church of England ceremony was also performed. There were periods when some nonconformists (Quakers for example) were allowed to marry in their own meeting houses but, even then, some couples thought it best to repeat the ceremony in a parish church (where the minister would allow it) in order to remove any possible question of illegitimacy, which of course might have affected inheritance.

The system of marrying by means of banns or by licence had applied since registers began, but after Hardwicke's Act of 1754, which called for separate books of registers to be kept for marriages, the reading of banns for all marriages other than those by licence was emphasised and from that time forward many parishes kept a separate banns book, many of which are still preserved today. Before 1754 few, if any, separate banns books exist.

Marriage by banns

Banns had to be read out in church on three successive Sundays to announce the intention to marry. This was in order to give anyone objecting to the marriage time to make his objection known. The banns were read in the churches of the bride and the groom, if they were from different parishes. This might mean that the banns entry could be found in a particular parish even though the marriage did not take place there. However as the parish of residence of the parties was almost always given, it should not be a problem locating the church of marriage once the banns have been found.

What this means in practice is that, assuming you have an idea of the date of your ancestor's marriage (say within ten years), even when the parish register fails to contain the marriage, you should search the banns book(s) for the parish, where you might well come across the marriage banns though the ceremony may have taken place in a quite unexpected parish fifty miles away. The existence of banns books will be recorded in the booklet from your County Record Office detailing surrendered parish registers, of which banns books form a part. The reading of banns in *both* parishes, where each of the couple was from a different parish, was not compulsory until 1823 but was often done nonetheless.

Another reason why the marriage entry might not be found is because some couples changed their minds and did not marry after all, even though the banns may have been read. So the existence of a banns entry does not necessarily mean the couple ultimately married; nor does the existence of a marriage licence, which we will come to shortly.

The entry for a marriage in the marriage register might repeat that information in the banns or might abbreviate the entry to just the names of the parties. You should always consult the banns book if there is reason to suppose the marriage was by that method. Any marriage not by licence had to be by banns. Since the licence system was more costly, the majority of ordinary people were married by banns – unless, for example, they had not had the required length of residence in the parish, or they wished to marry without waiting for three Sundays to pass, or they were both travelling some distance from home. As banns were normal for most marriages, the vicar would not always bother to specify this after the marriage entry. With a licence marriage, which was more unusual, he would be more likely to specify that licence was the method. No specification in the register of the method can almost always be taken to indicate that the marriage was by banns.

After 1837 marriage did not have to be in the established church, but could be, for example, at a registry office where banns were 'published' by means of a notice board. It is possible that before 1754 the reading of banns was not always adhered to; after 1754 it almost certainly was. The banns would normally state the marital status of the parties, which is especially important in the case of a widow or widower as far as your research is concerned. Parentage would not be mentioned in the banns unless one party should be a minor, when it might be.

Marriage by licence

Marriage licences were issued by the church authorities for those who did not wish to marry by the more public method of having the banns read out, or by those who for whatever reason wanted to marry hurriedly. As fees had to be paid to marry by licence it is likely that such a marriage is some indication of the financial status of the couple; certainly the poor would seldom have been married by licence.

A licence would be issued by the lowest rank of church official within whose jurisdiction both parties lived, or sometimes one of the parties only. This might be an Archdeacon, a Bishop, or an Archbishop, or a representative acting on behalf of one of these – that is a Chancellor or a surrogate. Certain parishes, known as Peculiars, might have licences issued by the clergyman of that parish.

Three documents were made out for a marriage by licence, though seldom today does more than one of the three survive. These were the *marriage allegation, the marriage bond*, and *the marriage licence*. Sometimes, even where none of the three survive today, a record may exist in the Act Book of the diocese. The documents relating to marriage by licence record no more than the intention to marry, and of course it sometimes happened that the couple changed their minds, so the existence of a bond, allegation or licence is not proof that a marriage ever took place. However, as you will usually be searching for one of these documents only *after* you have found the actual marriage entry in the parish register, this aspect is unlikely to affect you.

On the other hand if you have tried the likely parish registers and their banns books and failed to trace the marriage you seek, there is no reason why you should not try searching for a licence (most especially if these have been indexed for your locality and period) in the hope of locating it. To check on the availability and accessibility of marriage licences you need the book *Bishops' Transcripts and Marriage Licences, Bonds and Allegations* by Jeremy Gibson, published by the Federation of Family History Societies and regularly updated.

Licences were issued by any one of several tiers of the church authorities on an ascending scale, similar in manner to that of the probate courts (see page 102). Starting at the lowest level that scale of authorities ran as follows: the Parish Minister (only when that parish was a Peculiar); the Archdeacon; the Bishop; the Archbishop (of York or Canterbury). A Chancellor would issue the licence on behalf of an Archdeacon or Bishop, or a surrogate (official deputy) might act locally on behalf of a Chancellor. Just which authority (or deputy acting on his behalf) actually issued a licence would depend on whether either of the marrying couple or both of them or neither of them lived within the same diocese. Where a couple each lived in a different diocese within the Province of York, the authority was the Archbishop of York (through his Chancellor or surrogate of course). The Archbishop of Canterbury issued licences to marry in any parish within the Province of Canterbury through his Vicar-General. The Province of Canterbury was the senior of the two provinces and where a couple came from different provinces (or lived in one and wished to marry in the other) then the licence was issued by the Faculty Office of the Archbishop of Canterbury. Both the Faculty Office and the Vicar-General's Office were in London.

If this sounds complicated, then the reality is even more so. While this was the hierarchy of issuing authorities *in principle*, some couples appear to have gone to a higher authority than was necessary, perhaps for the same reasons that this happened with probate courts. Fortunately you do not need to worry about which licensing authority may have issued the licences you seek. Your local County Record Office (or other holding repository) will know all about ecclesiastical jurisdictions and will guide you to such indexes as exist. Those issued by the Faculty Office and the Vicar-General's Office are today at Lambeth Palace Library, London SE1 7JU, but some have been published and some copies of indexes are at the Society of Genealogists' Library. For full details see Gibson's book listed above.

The marriage licence itself was given to the couple to hand to the minister, who may have kept it in his parish chest for ever, returned it to the diocesan registry with other submissions, or thrown it away once he had examined it. There does not appear to have been any requirement for him to keep it. Very seldom will a licence survive today, and those that do seem to contain little detail, in fact nothing additional to that in the other documents which may survive, namely the allegation and the bond.

The marriage allegation was a statement sworn by one of the couple to state that there was no reason why they should not legally marry. Sometimes it was made by a relative or friend. In the case of minors the written consent of the parent was required. Allegations were discontinued after 1823.

Here is an allegation of 1787, a printed form onto which was handwritten the pertinent details.

The allegation reads as follows, the words in italic being those inserted by hand

On the *eighth* . . . . day of *December*
in the year of our Lord one thousand seven hundred and
eighty seven
Appeared personally *Randel Loomes, ffarmer and grazier*
. . . . . . and made oath that he is of
Husbands Bosworth . . . . . .
in the county of *Leicester* . . . . . . *aged Fifty* . . . .
. . . . years and a *Bachelor* . . . and intendeth
to marry with *Frances Brown of Husbands Bosworth*
aforesaid . . . . .
. . . . aged *fforty* . . . . . . years and a *widow* . . . .
And that he knoweth of no lawful impediment by reason of any
precontract, consanguinity, affinity, or any other lawful means

F

On the eighth . . . day of December –
in the year of our Lord one thousand seven hundred and
eighty seven.

Appeared personally Randel Loomes, Harmer and Grazier .
. . . . and made oath that he is of
Husbands Bosworth .
in the county of Leicester . . . . aged Fifty . .
. . years and a Bachelor . . . and intended .
to marry with Frances Brown of Husbands Bosworth
aforesaid . . . . . . —

aged Forty . . . years and a Widow . . .
And that he knoweth of no lawful impediment by reason of any
precontract, consanguinity, affinity, or any other lawful means
whatever to hinder the said intended marriage, and prayed a Licence
to solemnize the same in the parish church of Husbands
Bosworth aforesaid . . . .

And further made oath that the usual place of abode of the said
Frances Brown . . . . .
hath been in the said parish . . . . of Husbands
Bosworth . . . . . .

for the space of four weeks last past.

Randel Loomes

Sworn before me, Ph Hackett
Surrog ʸᵉ

Fig. 7.1 *Facsimile of marriage allegation of 1787.*

whatever to hinder the said intended marriage, and prayed a Licence
to solemnize the same in the *parish church of Husbands
Bosworth aforesaid* . . . .

And further made oath that the usual place of abode of *the said
Frances Brown* . . . .
hath been in the said *parish* . . . . . . of *Husbands Bosworth* . . . . . .
for the space of four weeks last past.

Randel Loomes.

Sworn before me, Ph Hackett

Surrogt.

The condition of each party (here bachelor and widow) is most
useful to the researcher, but the ages, while helpful, cannot be
relied on as accurate. Ages are especially unreliable when set in
such form as '21 years and upwards', which may mean no more
than 'of age', i.e., over 21.

The form of words of an allegation would vary in different regions,
but its intent was the same, and the details of the parties concerned
would be greater by far than the simple entry of marriage in the
registers. The same applies to the bond and its form of words and
while the information in the bond may be less detailed or more
detailed than that in the allegation, it too will be more helpful to
the genealogist than the marriage entry in the registers.

The marriage bond was a sworn statement, usually made by the
prospective groom and a friend (often of course a relative, thus
offering a further potential clue). The parties jointly bound themselves under risk of financial penalty to certify that there was no legal
impediment against the marriage. As with most bonds the mention
of a certain sum of money is *not* an indication that the parties had
such a sum at their disposal, so this is not an indication of wealth.
Sometimes, usually at a more recent time than an earlier period, the
second bondee was fictitious and no more than a formality. John Doe
was a well known invented name on such documents; Richard Roe
was another. The researcher needs to be cautious therefore and
not waste time trying to investigate the second bondee as a
potential relative when he may have been an invented signatory.

Fig. 7.2 (page 76) is a typical marriage bond – in fact the partner
to the allegation shown on page 74. In this example both allegation
and bond survive, though sometimes only one of the two may
have been preserved.

Again the bond is a printed form into which the appropriate
information is handwritten. The bond is in two sections; firstly what
is known as the obligation (which on earlier examples may be in
Latin), and secondly the condition, which is usually in English.

The wording of this bond reads as follows:

Know all men by these presents that Mr. *Randel Loomes
of Husbands Bosworth in the county of Leicester
ffarmer and grazier & William Jackson of the same
place ffarmer* . . . . . .
are held and firmly bound to *Edward Taylor Esqr.
B.L.L. official of the Archdeaconry of Leicester*

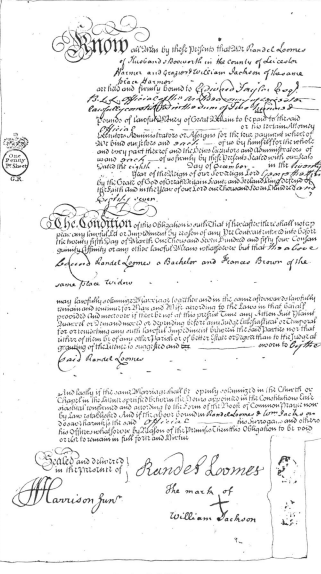

Fig. 7.2   *Facsimile of marriage bond of 1787.*

lawfully constituted in the sum of Two Hundred
pounds of lawful money of Great Britain to be paid to the said
official . . . . . . or his certain Attorney
Executors Administrators or Assigns for the true payment whereof
we bind ourselves and *each* . . . of us by himself for the whole
and every part thereof and the Heirs Executors and Administrators of
us and *each* . . . . of us firmly by these presents sealed with our seals
dated the *eighth* . . . . day of *December* . . . in the *twenty*
. . . *year of the reign of our Sovereign Lord George the third*
by the Grace of God of Great Britain and Ireland King defend of
the faith and in the year of our Lord one thousand seven hundred *and*
eighty seven.
The Condition of this obligation is such that if hereafter there shall
not ap-
pear any lawful Let of Impediment by reason of any pre contract
entered into before
the twenty fifth day of March One Thousand Seven Hundred and
fifty four Consan
guinity Affinity of any other lawful Means whatsoever but that
the above
bound Randel Loomes a Bachelor and Frances Brown of the
same place Widow . . . . . .
may lawfully solemnize marriage together and in the same afterwards
lawfully
remain and continue for Man and Wife according to the laws in that
behalf
provided And moreover if there be no at this present time any Action
Suit Plaint
Quarrel or Demand moved or depending before any Judge
Ecclesiastical or Temporal
for or concerning any such lawful Impediment between the said
Parties nor that
either of them be of any other Parish or of better Estate or Degree
than to the Judge of
granting of the Licence is suggested and . . . . . . sworn to *by the*
said Randel Loomes . . . . . .
. . . .
And lastly if the said Marriage shall be openly solemnized in the
Church or
Chapel in the Licence specified between the hours appointed in the
Constitutions Eccle
siastical confirmed and according to the form of the Book of Common
Prayer now
by law established And if the above bounden *Randel Loomes &*
Wm Jackson do save harmless the said *Official* . . . his Surrogate and
others his Officers whatsoever by reason of the premisis then this
Obligation to be void
or else to remain in full force and virtue.

Sealed and delivered	)	Randel Loomes
in the presence of	)	The mark of
		X

J. Harrison junr.

William Jackson

MISSING MARRIAGES

As you trace back your family tree, especially when you reach the period before about 1750, it is likely that certain marriages will be missing from your search results. Even though you may have followed your ancestral line back through two or three villages in the locality, you may find a marriage missing here and there. In other words, your ancestors did not marry in their own village churches. There are several possible reasons why this might be so, and of course you cannot anticipate the reason in any particular case. It has been estimated that somewhere between one in four and one in three marriages in the first half of the 18th century are 'missing' – missing that is from the places where they might be expected to be found, although more widespread searching might ultimately locate them. If you understand some of the reasons for this it may help you locate a missing marriage when the time comes.

Although the law specified that marriage was to be performed by a priest by banns or licence in a church of the parish of either of the marrying parties, any marriage was still legally binding even when not carried out under these circumstances. Ministers of some churches were lax in their application of the law, and this gave rise to the term 'lawless' churches. Some churches are recognised by genealogists as 'marrying' churches, where the number of marriages (before 1754) can be quite disproportionate to the population size, and it is obvious that such churches drew in couples from afar. Some might be couples 'running away' to marry against parental approval, especially if one party was under age. From 1754 Hardwicke's Act prevented such 'clandestine' marriages, sometimes known as 'irregular' marriages – or at least it went a long way towards doing so.

However the number of these (pre-1754) irregular marriages is such that a likely explanation for many of them was simply that some ministers offered a cut-price service and charged a lower fee. Also, by marrying away from home a couple would avoid the cost of the wedding celebration, which relatives and friends might otherwise expect them to hold. All the same there were ministers who would marry without asking too many questions – and without banns or licence. Often these would be ministers of 'Peculiar' parishes, as Peculiars often felt themselves to be free from ecclesiastical control to the extent as to be almost outside the law, or at least subject to their own version of the law.

Another magnet for couples marrying away from their home parishes was the larger towns, such as market towns, where a certain degree of anonimity might be offered to those looking for a quiet wedding. You should also bear in mind, if faced with the problem of missing marriages, that your ancestors may have married in a nonconformist chapel (or church or house), and, though it is unlikely that they would marry in nonconformity but baptise children in the parish church, it is nevertheless a possibility.

If you are faced with the problem of missing marriages in the provinces, especially in rural England before 1754, then likely places to search would be market towns and Peculiar parishes. However there was another major magnet for those marrying irregularly and that was London, where in 1700 one person in ten of the population lived anyway (in 1500 it was one person in fifty). Prior to 1754 there were over one hundred lawless churches in London, places where marriages were performed on the cheap and with no questions asked. The most notorious of these was the Fleet Chapel, where it is estimated that as many as 200,000 marriages took place before 1754. The registers of these are at the Public Record Office and a list of known lawless London churches is to be found in the National Index of Parish Registers, volume 1, by D. J. Steel, published by the Society of Genealogists.

Clandestine marriages post-1753

After 1753 these irregular marriages were drastically curtailed. Though there were still runaway couples, of course, they now had to run to some marrying parish outside the control of English law, and that meant, principally, Scotland, where Gretna Green is the most famous centre for clandestine marriages. Such marriages could, and did, take place at any parish in Scotland without formalities, but Gretna was conveniently close to the border and was easy of access by a regular coach road. Scottish law was not sufficiently changed until the mid-19th century to stop this practice. The Isle of Man and the Channel Islands were also places of refuge for those wishing to marry away from parental control.

Whether you are seeking a regular marriage or a clandestine one there are today many aids towards simplifying the task in the form of indexes. The most obvious, already mentioned, is the IGI, itself a massive index to marriages as well as baptisms and burials. Another massive index is known as *Boyd's Marriage Index*, located at the Society of Genealogists and containing over seven million names (many culled from published parish registers). The *Pallot Index* is held by the Institute of Heraldic and Genealogical Studies, Canterbury, and is especially helpful for post-1780 London marriages.

In recent years numerous marriage indexes have been (and are still being compiled by individuals and local family history groups. Most such indexes are no more than that, and will not give the full information to be found in the original registers. Some are indexed by male name only. Nevertheless these are very convenient mechanisms towards locating the parish involved. To learn what indexes exist you should consult J. S. W. Gibson's *Marriage, Census and Other Indexes for Family Historians* published by the Federation of Family History Societies.

8 NONCONFORMISTS AND IMMIGRANTS

Nonconformity began, as far as genealogy is concerned, with Henry VIII's break with the church of Rome in 1534, when he appointed himself head of the Church of England (sometimes referred to as the Anglican Church or the Episcopalian Church). Those who refused to conform to the national religion were persecuted by fine or imprisonment or both. The keeping of records of the activities of their members would have been dangerous and few Nonconformist groups have surviving records before the second half of the 18th century, when attitudes had modified. ('Nonconformism' is a term used to describe all religious denominations outside the Church of England.) It is possible that some earlier records were kept secretly and hidden away, and it is impossible for us to know today whether the records of some groups were never kept at all or have been lost. Notable exceptions were the Quakers, whose records are often well preserved from the second half of the 17th century.

With the start of Civil Registration in 1837 the government attempted to centralise the holdings of the many widespread records of the Nonconformists, and in the following few years most such records were handed in and today are housed in the Public Record Office. For the reasons stated above it is difficult to know how many registers may have escaped being surrendered. It is also likely that some registers are incomplete and it is a well-known fact that Nonconformist records for a particular chapel may commence at a later date than the founding of the chapel, perhaps because earlier volumes have been lost.

Numerous problems face the genealogist with ancestors who were Nonconformists. Firstly you might not know when you begin tracing your family tree that your ancestors *were* Nonconformists. Even if you do know that some of them were Nonconformists of a particular sect, you may find that they changed their allegiance between different faiths at differrent times, though this is less likely with Roman Catholic and Jewish families, where religion was strongly enforced. A present-day family following the Quaker religion is also likely to find that its ancestors were Quakers far back in time. An Anglican family may on the other hand find past members who turned to Quakerism for short periods, and this can come as a surprise.

For most people it is likely that thoughts of Nonconformity within the family will only arise when the records of the established church fail to produce the expected results. At that time you may wish to search for the required events in Nonconformist records and you will not be able to guess in advance which of the many denominations may apply – though you may decide to exclude Catholic and Jewish records as family memory tends not to forget membership of these more distinctive faiths. All other denominations, including Quakers, are groups to which Anglican ancestors may have turned at some time or other, even if only for a short period in the life of one ancestor – and of course such a short period may be just what you need to bridge a gap in what might otherwise be a continuous pedigree.

We will come shortly to the nomenclature of the many varied and confusing groups of Nonconformists, but regardless of what type of Nonconformity was involved, certain conditions pertained to them all. From the start of parish registers (1538) it was the duty of the minister of the parish throughout almost the entire period up to the start of the 19th century to record in his registers the events of his parishioners, *whether they were Nonconformists or not*. In practice this hardly ever happened, even though periodic instructions were submitted to emphasise this duty. The parish register was the only recorded evidence to prove birth, marriage or death of parishioners – even though it was the baptism that was recorded rather than the birth for most of the period in question. A parish register entry was, and still is, legal evidence, something which could be vital to prove legitimacy if an inheritance was involved.

Some ministers recorded events in the lives of Nonconformists faithfully throughout their period of office, though perhaps the previous and succeeding ones did not. Sometimes these events would be on a separate page or two of the register and designated as relating to Nonconformists. Sometimes they would be amongst the other entries, sometimes with distinction made and sometimes not. Many Nonconformists did not baptise children and in such cases a dutiful minister might still record the birth of their children. At all times it was the minister's duty to marry parishioners in church, but some refused outright to marry people they regarded as non-believers, and some refused to bury them in what they regarded as holy ground (but might carry out the burial in some ground outside the churchyard proper, and set aside for that purpose).

Another reason why Nonconformist events seldom appear in a parish register is because the group themselves refused to attend church or to partake in its ceremonies. Instead they might have carried out their own marriage ceremony (though illegal) and might have buried their dead in their own burial grounds, as the Quakers often did in the garden or orchard of a house used for meetings, which was quite lawful and still is!

WERE YOUR ANCESTORS NONCONFORMISTS?
So as you progress in tracking back your Anglican ancestry, your first suspicions of Nonconformity within your family could be aroused by the absence of entries, by the presence of entries specifically denoting your ancestor as Nonconformist, or by the

presence of entries alongside others but worded differently, or set on a page apart from the rest.

For example if your ancestor's entries relate to the *birth* of children, when those alongside relate to baptism, this is often a pointer to Nonconformity. If your ancestor is 'interred' rather than 'buried' this can also be an indication, though there is always a chance that a particular clerk may have described them all as 'interred'. Some even described a Nonconformist corpse as being 'thrown into the ground' or by some other derogatory expression.

Many ministers used terms bordering on abuse to describe Nonconformists in their registers, or even terms of real abuse. Very often however they would use some term to indicate Nonconformity, which might be an accurate term referring to the actual faith, for instance, Quaker or Roman Catholic. Or it might be a definitive term used inaccurately or loosely in a generic manner, such as Dissenter, Anabaptist, Presbyterian, and you must be careful not to interpret the terminology used in parish registers in describing Nonconformists as accurately defining the particular Nonconformist sect. The term 'Recusant' usually refers to Roman Catholics but can at times be used to mean no more than Nonconformist. The term Popish Recusant is almost always an indication of Roman Catholicism. You must always be wary of taking at face value any reference to Nonconformity by a parish minister.

The record of marriage was especially important in proving legitimacy of children, and some members of Nonconformist sects might go through two ceremonies: one in the parish church and one in their own place of worship under their own ceremonies. Hardwicke's Act of 1754 enforced the existing law that all marriages had to be performed within the Church of England, though Jews and Quakers were exempted and thereafter their own records were considered valid. Some Roman Catholics still defied the Act.

So at the point where you might turn to Nonconformist records you will approach from one of two possible standpoints. You might already know that your family were, and perhaps still are, Nonconformists, in which case you will want to turn to those records of the recognised denomination once you know how to locate those which are close to your area of interest geographically. The second standpoint is that you will begin by not knowing which sect, if any, your family followed and you will want to search the Nonconformist records (known as non-parochial registers) that are closest in location and time to your genealogical problem – excluding, in the first instance, the records of Catholics, Jews and Huguenots (see page 84). At the outset at least, you are not so much concerned with what each Nonconformist group believed as with where they had their meetings and what records they left behind. A good idea is to begin by plotting onto a map of the area of your interest those chapels known to have existed and to have left records. A one-inch Ordnance Survey map is fine for this purpose.

The Public Record Office has a list of non-parochial registers surrendered and this is set out on a county basis. You need a copy of this list. Your local County Record Office will have a copy, so will the libraries of many larger towns, the Mormon Family History libraries, and the Society of Genealogists, but it may be more convenient for you to have photocopies made from that nearest you, or easiest of access. Your local County Record Office may also be aware of other non-parochial registers, perhaps including some *not* deposited in the Public Record Office, and they may even hold some themselves.

Bear in mind that Nonconformist preachers often covered a very wide territory, usually known as a circuit. They may have held meetings at several widely-spread places while recording events in a register at only one place as a sort of centralised recording system for the circuit. This means that the name by which the register is known may be misleading, so spread your net wide in plotting chapels onto your map.

Having charted the location of the chapels with registers, you will want to search them one by one in the same way that you searched parish registers. Microfilm copies exist of the non-parochial registers at the Public Record Office, and copies will be available at the Mormon Family History libraries, at some County Record Offices or local libraries within your area. Also of course entries from these registers may well be included in the IGI, so perhaps that should be first on your search list, or at least you could establish which ones are included for your area.

The Quakers, strictly known as Friends from their correct title as the Society of Friends, have well-kept records of births, marriages and burials which extend for many areas to the mid-17th century. Digests of these are kept at the Library of the Society of Friends, Friends House, Euston Road, London NW1 2BJ. Public access is permitted and a search fee is charged. The Society of Genealogists have published a booklet *My Ancestors were Quakers: how can I find out more about them?* The majority of Quaker registers were surrendered, though not absolutely all, but, prior to surrendering, 'digests' (summarised copies) were made and indexed. These digests may fail to include all the information in the originals in the Public Record Office, and in any event will not include entries from registers which have come to light since surrendering. Local Record Offices often have minutes of the meetings (held monthly, quarterly and yearly) and these may give considerable background information over and above that in the registers.

Quakers seem not to have been daunted by the difficulties of travel and, even in the 17th century and early 18th, would often visit other groups of Friends at great distance (including America). Often they would send a Friend with a letter of introduction to a distant meeting and, where marriage took place between a couple from widespread areas, considerable detail may be recorded in the minutes. Information in the minutes in some ways resembles that found in Settlement Certificates (see page 126), and so these can be a rich source of detail seldom available in Anglican records.

Catholicism was stronger in Northern England than in the South and stronger among the gentry than in the labouring classes. Entries for baptisms, marriages and burials are sometimes found in Anglican registers, those involved often being denoted as Papists or Popish Recusants. Some children were baptised 'privately', probably in the house of the parents, and were perhaps entered in the registers with the tolerance of the Anglican minister without reference to the fact that the baptism had not been in Anglican form. However private baptism was practised in Anglican families too at times, so this is not a definite indication of Catholicism. Some ministers refused to allow burial of the unbaptised, and private burial *at night* by the family was sometimes allowed, possibly outside the churchyard itself. Night-time burial is an almost certain sign of Catholicism.

Registers of Catholic ceremonies, if kept at all, were often hidden away and many must have been lost. Most surviving Catholic registers date from no earlier than the second half of the 18th century, often later. Many have been published by the Catholic Record Society (114 Mount Street, London W1Y 6AH) and are available in most larger libraries. Catholics largely refused to surrender their registers to the government repository (now the Public Record Office) and some are still with the churches while others have more recently been deposited in local County Record Offices. The Catholic Family History Society is based at 2 Winscombe Crescent, Ealing, London W5 1AZ (Mrs. B. Murray). If researching a Catholic family you should read *Sources for Roman Catholic and Jewish Genealogy and Family History* by D. J. Steel, being volume 3 in the National Index of Parish Registers published for the Society of Genealogists.

When we come to Protestant Nonconformists there were many minority sects, some of which joined forces at certain times, and others subdivided at other times. The Baptists were one major group whose records were surrendered. The Methodists were another and they split into several lesser groups such as Wesleyan Methodists, Primitive Methodists, Methodist New Connexion, Bible Christians, and others. Most records of Methodists and Baptists were surrendererd, and will appear on the list of non-parochial registers now at the Public Record Office, as mentioned earlier, and many of these register entries will now appear in the IGI. The Society of Genealogists have published *My Ancestors were Baptists: how can I find out more about them?* and *My Ancestors were Methodists: how can I find out more about them?* – essential reading if your ancestry belonged to these denominations.

Another major Protestant Nonconformist denomination, known as Congregationalists (and also as Independents) joined together in 1972 with the Presbyterian and Unitarian churches to form the United Reformed Church. The United Reformed Church Historical

Society, 86 Tavistock Place, London WC1H 9RT, is an amalgamation of what were formerly the Congregational Historical Society and the Presbyterian Historical Society. Records of all these denominations were also surrendered, and are now at the Public Record Office, and included in the IGI. Those records surrendered by what was classed together as the Three Denominations (Presbyterians, Independents and Baptists) included a register of births begun in 1742 at Dr Williams's Library in London and containing some 50,000 entries, mostly from London but some from* elsewhere. The Wesleyan Methodists began a General Registry in 1818 at Paternoster Row, London, to record births and baptisms, mostly from London but some from elsewhere, and this record contains some 10,000 entries.

Those researching Nonconformist ancestors (other than Catholics and Jews) should refer to *Sources for Nonconformist Genealogy and Family History* by D. J. Steel, published for the Society of Genealogists as volume 2 of the National Index of Parish Registers.

Microfilm copies exist of all the non-parochial registers mentioned above and held at the Public Record Office. These may well be available at local Record Offices and the Mormon Family History Libraries, and perhaps also at some larger town libraries.

WERE YOUR ANCESTORS IMMIGRANTS?

Great Britain has always acted as a magnet in drawing in immigrants and many British families today have immigrant ancestors, though may be quite unaware of that fact since many names once foreign have become Anglicised over the generations. Even such a commonplace name as Brown may have originated here in the 16th century as De Bruijne, Walwin as Vallin, and some are readily recognisable ones such as Bogarde and Bogart, Bosanquet, etc. So whether or not you begin your research expecting your ancestors to have originated in France or the Low Countries, you may well find before long that you will need to turn to such records as will help you track down immigrants.

Those researching Nonconformist ancestors (other than Catholics and Jews) should refer to *Sources for Nonconformist Genealogy and Family History* by D. J. Steel, published for the Society of Genealogists as volume 2 of the National Index of Parish Registers.

Microfilm copies exist of all the non-parochial registers mentioned above and held at the Public Record Office. These may well be available at local Record Offices and the Mormon Family History Libraries, and perhaps also at some larger town libraries. businessmen often to do with the wool or cloth trade.

However there had been considerable numbers of French, Belgian, Dutch and even German craftsmen who had come to England at a much earlier time, at the end of the 16th and beginning of the 17th centuries. Many of these came here to exploit the ready market offered, principally in London, for crafts in which they excelled. So great was the problem of 'foreign' craftsmen working in London to the detriment of the native tradesmen that the London City Companies originated protective guilds to keep outsiders from taking trade from those already established there. Several of the City Companies of handcraft workers originated at the beginning of the 17th century with this as one of their objectives. Clockmakers, watchmakers, engravers, goldsmiths and jewellers formed a considerable number of these immigrants.

In the early days they tended to group together in certain districts of London and in other towns, principally Norwich, Colchester, Bristol, Exeter and Plymouth. They retained their own language among themselves even though they learned to speak English too. Often they had their own churches and the records were recorded either in Latin or in their original language. Like many immigrants they traded amongst themselves and married from within their own kind until gradual assimilation into the native population took place. The original small but thriving communities were expanded considerably after 1685 by the influx of many further religious refugees, and these newcomers also gravitated to areas where their countrymen were already settled, some of whom would be kinfolk and business associates. They attended their own places of worship, which became known as Dutch churches or French churches, even though their members may not have been strictly from France or Holland.

The Huguenot Society has published records for many years in connection with the history and genealogy of these immigrants, and numerous volumes are in print concerning Returns of Aliens, lists of Denizens (foreigners settled here) and registers of Dutch, French and Walloon churches in England. The Huguenot Library is at University College, Gower Street, London WC1E 6BP. Several books exist concerning Huguenot ancestry – see Appendix D, the bibliography.

If you suspect your name may be of Huguenot origin, or if other searches lead you to consider that possibility; or even if you are just prospecting around for earlier examples of your surname at a time when you have lost your genealogical trail, then a glance at the indexes of a few volumes of the Huguenot Society's publications (available in many large libraries) may resolve the problem.

The original registers of these churches were surrendered with non-parochial registers in general and are now at the Public Record Office. Most, if not all, have been published by the Huguenot Society, address c/o Huguenot Library). These published works are all indexed but you need to watch out for erratic spellings far more carefully than with English-name registers.

Some years ago I was researching the ancestry of Ahasuerus Fromanteel, the first man in England to make pendulum clocks (in 1658). He was known to be of Flemish origin ultimately and to have come to London from Norwich in the 1630s. This at first looked impossible as the early registers of the Dutch Church at Norwich were lost. However it proved that they had been published before being lost, and this shows just how important transcripts can be, of whatever nature. In some local records the name Fromanteel appeared in such Anglicised versions as Frummity (one can imagine it said with a Norfolk accent) and Freemantle (probably only a mis-reading of Fromantle). The vital entry was eventually found and was a mixture of Latinisations and 17th-century Dutch, reading:

> 1606/07. Assuwerus fromateel, filius Mardochens end Lea, Gheboren den 25e februaij en gedoopt den 8e martij: get Boudewijn fromanteel, Josias valcke, ende Abigael fromateel.

The occasional appearance of Fromanteel as Fromateel probably indicates that the transcriber missed a small abbreviation sign over the a to indicate the n was omitted. The entry translates as:

> Ahasuerus, son of Murdoch and Lea(h), born 25th February, baptised 8th March: witnesses Baldwin Fromanteel, Josiah Valck and Abigail Fromanteel.

Jews in Britain were both Nonconformists and immigrants, although some Jewish families have lived here over 300 years. Jews were expelled from Britain in 1290 but during the Commonwealth (1655 in fact) they were again permitted to settle here, largely to escape persecution in their European homelands. The Jews who came to Britain in the 17th century and those who came here in general before the late 19th century, came principally from Portugal and are known as Sephardic Jews, a word which comes from medieval Hebrew and means 'Spaniards'. These were often the aristocracy of the Jewish world and included many who were merchants and traders. During this long period of settlement here the Sephardic Jews became integrated into the native population, though still retained their own religion. Even so some Jewish entries can be found in parish registers. London was the principal place of residence of Jews before the 19th century.

The other major phase of Jewish immigrants came to Britain from Eastern Europe (Russia, Poland and Rumania) and are known as Ashkenazi Jews from the medieval Hebrew word meaning 'Germans'. They came mostly in the latter part of the 19th century and were often from much poorer backgrounds. Jewish organisations here helped these impoverished settlers during their initial period of settlement. By the early 19th century there were considerable Jewish communities in the major provincial towns as well as in London.

One problem with Jewish genealogy is the instability of names, or at least of the names they adopted here. The patronymic method of naming (Isaac ben Israel = Isaac, son of Israel) sometimes modified to Isaac Israels, still patronimic but using a genitive 's', but was prone to changing at each generation. Sometimes a different name was used for trade purposes. The Ashkenazi Jews tended to Anglicise their names either by abbreviation (Finkelstein might become Stein or even Anglicised to Stone) or by straight translation. An example often quoted of the latter is the Hebrew name Zevi (a stag) Germanised to Hirsch, then Anglicised to Hart. Jacobson might go unrecognised when translated to Jackson.

Jewish records were generally well kept and well preserved. Records may be still with the synagogue, but some are at The Jewish Museum, Woburn House, Upper Woburn Place, London WC1H 0EP. There is now a Jewish Historical Society at 33 Seymour Place, London W1H 5AP.

The Society of Genealogists has published a booklet, *My Ancestor was Jewish: how can I find out more about him?* Those with Jewish ancestry should consult *Sources for Roman Catholic and Jewish Genealogy and Family History* by D. J. Steel, published as volume 3 in the National Index of Parish Registers by the Society of Genealogists.

When you first begin to search parish registers, whether the originals or transcripts of any kind, you are likely to come across certain things which may at first look puzzling, though you will very soon become accustomed to them. One of these is the use of Latin, not in its own right but more in the form of Latinisations of such things as names.

LATINISATION

Surnames were hardly ever Latinised, even if an entry should have been written entirely in Latin. You are unlikely to come across Latin or Latinisations in your first searches. Latin was seldom used in parish registers later than about 1700 and your initial searches will be in a much more recent period than that. So until you are using registers dated before 1700, or even earlier, you are unlikely to see Latin or even Latinised first names, and when you do come across them, most are fairly obvious even to someone who never saw a word of Latin before. Edward for example is Latinised to *Edwardus*, Robert to *Robertus*, Francis to *Franciscus,* Frances (female) to *Francesca*. Even if the Latin endings may be unfamiliar, the root of the name is clear enough.

Although Latin names are seldom found in such records as parish registers before the early 18th century, they might well be used in such documents as a bond. In that case there will often be an English version alongside the Latin, so that again no problem is likely to defeat you.

Parish registers having Latinised entries will often use the genitive form, meaning 'of'. This is confusing if it is new to you but very easy to get used to. For instance '3 Jul 1673 Bap. *Edwardus filius Roberti Smith*' means that the child baptised was Edward son of Robert Smith. The masculine *-us* ending is changed to *-i* in the genitive and *-ius* to *-ii*, for instance, *Georgii*. The female ending *-a* changes in the genitive to *-ae* to produce such an entry as '3 Jul 1673 Bap. *Edwardus filius Roberti et Francescae Smith*'!

A few Latin forms of first names are rather different from the English. Some of the less obvious ones are:

Aegidius – Giles	*Aloysius* – Lewis
Carolus – Charles	*Dionysius* – Denis
Galfridus – Geoffrey	*Galterus* – Walter
(or *Gaufridus*)	(or *Gawtherus*)
Guido – Guy	*Gulielmus* – William
Hieremias – Jeremiah	*Hieronymus* – Jerome
Jacobus – James *or* Jacob	*Johanna* – Joan/Jane/Jean/Janet
Johannes – John	*Lionhardus* – Leonard

Ludovicus – Lewis   *Radulphus* – Ralph
Umfridus – Humphrey

During the period when parish register entries were in Latin, certain words recur frequently. The most common of these are set out below.

adulter – adulterer   *adultera* – adulteress
aetatis – aged (i.e., being of the age of, followed by the number)
agricola – farmer   *alias* – otherwise known as
apud – at (a particular place)   *armiger* – one with a coat of arms (knight)
civis – citizen   *coelebs* – single person
defunctus – deceased   *dies* – day
die – on that day   *eodem* – the same (*oedem die* – on the same day)
femina – woman   *filia* – daughter
filius – son   *filii* – children
frater – brother   *gemellae* – female twins
gemelli – male twins   *homo* – man
infans – infant   *mater* – mother
mens – month   *mensis* – of the month (e.g., day of)
mortuus – dead (man)   *mortua* – dead (woman)
mulier – woman   *nuper* – formerly of, late of
obiit – he died   *parochia* – parish
pater – father   *pater familias* – householder
puella – girl   *puer* – boy
relicta – widow (relict)   *relictus* – widower
renatus – baptised   *requiescat in pace* – rest in peace
senex – old man   *sepultus* – buried
soror – sister   *testamentum* – will
ultimo die – on the last day   *uxor* – wife
vidua – widow

ABBREVIATIONS

Latinisation alone is not often a problem. Unfortunately for the beginner the clerks of the day would often use abbreviations just to shorten the tedious task of writing down names all day long. Abbreviation was used not only for names but for numerous commonplace words too, and a novice today meeting abbreviations, and perhaps Latinisation too, with the combined problem that the writing is faded or the ink adhered imperfectly to the slightly greasy surface of parchment or vellum, may feel baffled. It will help if the abbreviation system is understood first, before applying it to names.

At first abbreviations may seem a rather random affair, but there was a recognised system and method of abbreviating, although each individual clerk's method may have varied from that of the next one and may, in any event, have been inconsistent. Once you know the basic concept of abbreviating, the recognition of abbreviated words is usually straightforward.

Perhaps the most common sign of abbreviation is a short wavy line placed above the letter immediately before the omitted ones. Thus 'p̃ish' is short for 'parish', the ~ signifying omission of the letters 'ar'. Such an omission symbol could indicate any number of missing letters and any letters, often in a word including 'ion'. Thus 'adm̃on' for 'administration'.

Some clerks might place the wavy line through a letter, such as the downstroke of a p. Some might use an apostrophe instead, as in 'p'fect' for 'perfect'. Some might fail to put any abbreviation mark at all. You will very soon get used to abbreviated words and for the great majority of first-timers you can usually guess what word is intended by the abbreviated form, with or without an indication mark.

First names were often abbreviated, and these are much the same as we might use today. 'Ric' or 'Ricd' or 'Richd' are all obviously Richard. Those which might just confuse the beginner are 'Josh', which is almost always short for Joseph not Joshua. Joseph might just appear as 'Joph', but beware that an occasional clerk might just have written 'Josh' for Joshua.

The beginner might be confused by 'Jno', which was often used for John, and not for Jonathan. In older scripts, both hand-written and printed (as in books or printed forms), a capital I was often interchanged for J. John or Joseph might be written as Iohn or Ioseph, and might therefore appear abbreviated as Ino. or Iosh. This I for J could apply to any name, so that James Jackson could be written as Iames Iackson or shortened to Ias.Iackson. On the other hand, J could *not* be used instead of I and a name such as Ivison could not appear as Jvison. This interchangeability of I for J poses no problem once you are aware of it, except perhaps in a name such as Ianson, which might be confused with the name Janson – either could be written as Ianson.

The abbreviation 'Edwd.' for Edward might be confused with 'Edmd.' for Edmund. In practice the name Edmund was not a popular one until we get back to the 17th century, at which time, oddly enough, the two names often appear to have been used interchangeably.

To return to our Latinised entry, we might come across this in abbreviated form as '3 Jul 1673 Bap. *Edūs fil Robti Smith*', and this might appear without the abbreviation marks as a clue to the missing letters. Even so it does not take long to recognise this as *'Edwardus filius Roberti Smith'*. Some are less easy to spot. *'Gul. fil Rici Smith'* (*Gulielmus filius Richardi Smith* – William son of Richard Smith).

Surnames were not often abbreviated and when they were the

abbreviation is usually a very obvious one such as 'Sand'son' for Sanderson. As surnames were frequently spelt phonetically anyway, these are unlikely to catch you out.

A few short and commonplace words were often abbreviated. Y^e is a familiar one for 'the'. Here the Y is a sign representing the old 'th' sound and, even though written as Y, was pronounced as 'th'. Similarly Y^t is short for that. W^{ch} and W^{th} are short for which and with, and in these shortenings the second part of the word was often written above the base line of the rest of the lettering. 'Y^e letter y^t ye sent me' would be pronounced 'The letter that ye sent me'. As you work back slowly in time you will gradually grow used to such abbreviations until you are scarcely aware of them.

Sometimes an X was used as an abbreviation of Christ in just the same way that we sometimes today write Xmas. 'Xtian burial' is clearly 'Christian burial' but less immediately obvious is Xtopher or even Xtofer for Christopher, and this can appear as Xpoper. Such an odd entry as Xtofer Xtie would be Christopher Christie!

FIRST NAMES

First names went through periods of fashion, just as they do today. Names such as Elvis, Ringo, Shane, Duane were virtually unknown until the rise of the heroes after whom children are named today. In past centuries our ancestors had just the same attitudes towards naming their children after their idols – religious figures, folk heroes, classical heroes, kings or queens, and (especially in Puritan times) virtues. For much of the historical period you will be dealing with however, there was always a strong inclination to name children from within the family, and it will often be found that naming patterns recur. This is seldom obvious when the names used are names which are common anyway – John, Henry, William, James, etc. But where a family included names which were less commonplace – Ralph, Roger, Clement, Hugo, for instance – it does not take you long to become aware that some first names will repeat generation after generation.

The reasons for this repetition of names are not entirely known. It might first seem that a couple might name the first son after the man's father (sometimes the wife's father), first daughter after the mother (of either), and so on, and this does seem a very likely reason. However it is sometimes argued that such naming was after godparents, who would in any case tend to be uncles or aunts, sisters, etc. Whatever the reason, a regular crop of names occurring in unusual combination can very often be a guide towards identifying your family from a group of others in the locality having the same surname.

With the high mortality rate among young children, this naming pattern is seen to be even more obvious and determined. The first child, Robert, might have died within a year or two, perhaps after the second child, Janet, has been born. The third child, a boy, may very well have been named Robert again. The first girl, Janet, perhaps died, and then the next girl might again be named Janet. Names were often repeated in this way to the point where it is soon apparent that the couple were determined to have a Robert and a Janet, and so on.

In Puritan times there was a strong inclination towards names of virtue – Charity, Mercy, Faith, Hope, Prudence, and surprisingly some of these were at times used for boys as well as girls. At all times there were occasional eccentrics who named their issue in ways bordering on the ridiculous. Mark Anthony Dempster was a clockmaker working in Richmond, Yorkshire, in the mid-19th century. Amongst his children were: Mark Anthony, Julius Caesar, and Marcus Brutus. Another of his children, born in 1843, was named Gafee, and illustrates yet another naming system, that of using a surname as a first name. Another clockmaker working in Richmond at this same time was John Gafee Shirton, his middle name being almost certainly a local surname. If a John Richards married Mary Stanhope they may well have named one child Stanhope Richards, to carry on the female surname. Such an unusual first name may well serve as a clue to a female maiden name.

One first name was normal for most people at most periods. The practice of having two (or even more) first names was not common in any but the upper classes until the start of the 19th century. A very strange practice which you may come across was that of naming more than one living child with the *same* name. It was, fortunately, an uncommon practice and was usually confined to the period before about 1600, often the second half of the 16th century. If you encounter this without being aware of the practice, it can prove very puzzling. A man named Ralph Blenkinsop, may have decided to name his first son Roger, his second son also Roger and even a third son by the same name. When he died his will might describe them as his oldest son Roger, his middle son Roger and his youngest son Roger.

A few names were either regarded as interchangeable or as being the familiar and regular forms of the same name. It is sometimes difficult to know which. For instance a girl named at baptism as Margaret might be known amongst her family by the familiar forms of Peg or Peggy or perhaps Meg. When the census clerk asked the girl's name he may have been told the name by which the family knew her – Peggy for instance – yet a search for her ancestry would fail to show a Peggy and would show a Margaret. This does not pose a problem provided you know that Peggy is the familiar form of Margaret.

One of the more confusing can be Ann(e), which may appear as Anna, and may be interchanged with Hannah. In older periods (perhaps pre-1650) the form Annis (sometimes Annys or Annais) was sometimes used for Ann, but also for Agnes. To some extent therefore this group of names is often no more than a spelling variation for the same name. Esther and Hester were usually interchangeable, as were Mary Anne and Marian(ne). So too were Joan and Jane, and Jane's diminutives Janet or Jennett and Jenny.

Old name forms which you may at first fail to recognise are: Barnard for Bernard, Dionys for Denis, Ra(y)fe or Raphe for Ralph, and Symond for Simon.

Diminutive and pet forms of first names which may be unfamiliar are:

> Aggie for Agnes
> Bess, Bessie, Betsy, Betty for Elizabeth
> Dolly for Dorothy
> Eliza for Elizabeth
> Fanny for Frances
> Jenny for Jane/Janet
> Lizzie for Elizabeth
> Lottie for Charlotte
> Molly for Mary
> Nancy or Nanny (even Nan) for Ann
> Nell or Nellie for Eleanor (or Ellen or Helen)
> Rena or Renie for Irene

Your familiarity with the wide variety of given names will increase rapidly with experience. After a while you may be able to see some sort of pattern in the given names of your own ancestors. Different regions of the country had their own local preferences, however, and what at first might seem to be a helpful combination of repeated names (suggesting clues as to the direction of your research) might turn out to be a false lead. I can distinctly recall one search where the name Emanuel cropped up repeatedly, which at first seemed helpful as that is not a commonplace name. On another occasion the names Lawrence and Leonard kept occurring in the same family. It did not take long however to notice that these given names, unusual though they might be in general, reappeared time and time again in those parishes – and in many other families besides the one I was tracing.

Sometimes first names can be a clue towards the religious inclinations of the families, though this is seldom easy for the novice to spot. The first names Vincent and Anthony often occur in Catholic families, as do Peter and Joseph, but then these names may occur elsewhere too.

TITLES AND SOCIAL DISTINCTIONS

Some of the terms used to describe people both in parish registers and in certain other documents may be unfamiliar. A *Gentleman* originally signified one who had the right to a coat of arms (i.e., was armigerous), though by the early 19th century had come to mean a person of some social standing. An *Esquire* may have signified a member of a landowning family, probably of lesser status than a Gentleman, but was also used for those holding office under the Crown, such as a Justice of the Peace. The distinctions as to who was a Gentleman and who an Esquire were often blurred, depending on the period and on the person's attitude who wrote down the information.

The term *Master*, ultimately abbreviated to *Mr*, signified a person of social standing. The word *Mistress*, abbreviated to *Mrs*, apart from the wife of a Master, was also a term denoting a lady of the higher social orders, but was also used for a spinster of that status. You must therefore avoid falling into the trap of seeing a marriage entry of Mr James Talltrees to Mrs Emily Radcliffe and assuming that the lady was a widow, for she may well have been single. The term *Miss* was used for unmarried ladies, usually of some social standing, from about the middle of the 18th century. However, just to complicate things, when a Miss reached her more senior years, she was sometimes referred to as Mrs in the respectful sense of Mistress, even though she was unmarried. So you should always note such a title as Mrs or Miss, as these may denote social standing or respect, but beware that they may, or may not mean the same thing as they do today. When plain John Brown married plain Mary Higgins the parish registers would write their names and perhaps no more. Any mention of Mr, Mrs or Miss suggests that someone held them in greater than average esteem.

The term *Widow* mostly meant just that, but not always. Sometimes a lady of independent means and generally of advanced years might be termed 'Widow Johnson' or 'Widow Braithwaite' when she had always been a spinster. A parish register entry such as: 'Buried 18 March 1753 Griselda Johnson, widow.' probably means just that. An entry reading: 'Buried 18 March 1753 Widow Johnson' might or might not. Jot any phrase down as part of the entry, but do not always take it at face value.

The term *Yeoman* referred to a man who cultivated his own land; some were well-to-do but others were not. A *Husbandman* was a man who cultivated land which he rented, and was usually therefore less prosperous than a Yeoman. The two terms were not always used with any clearly-intended distinction one from the other, and at times these were interchangeable expressions. Sometimes a Husbandman meant little more than a householder. A *Citizen* was not the same thing as we might mean today by a citizen. Usually this word was used in conjunction with the man's trade, particularly in wills and other documents rather than in parish registers. 'Thomas Cartwright, Citizen and Clockmaker' meant a man who was a freeman of the Worshipful Company of Clockmakers (of London). 'Citizen' signified his rank or qualification. He might or might not have practised the trade of a clockmaker, as there were several reasons why people were sometimes allowed to join a particular company even though they followed a quite different trade.

A *Relict* is a word seldom seen today except in old parish

registers and probate records and means the one left behind when a married partner dies. It could relate to a man but normally signifies his widow. 'Buried 8 June 1634 the Relict of Thomas Jones', would be the sort of entry, or perhaps '8 June 1634 buried Janet, Relict of Thomas Jones.' The point about either entry is that Thomas Jones himself had died some time previously.

10   WILLS 1 – HOW TO LOCATE THEM

Wills are probably the most interesting, informative and exciting records you will uncover about your family. If you wonder how a will can be exciting, this will very soon become apparent to you once you handle the first will you find of your own ancestor. You will be holding a piece of paper first held by your ancestor perhaps two, three, or more centuries ago. What is written down there is what *he* told the clerk to write. At the end of it you will see *his* signature, or perhaps his mark if he could not write, and perhaps also his seal. The signatures of other close relatives may also appear. A will is probably the closest physical contact you will have with your ancestor and it is more than likely that this document has never been examined, never been read by anyone else since the day it was filed away for safe keeping.

You may expect a will to disclose information concerning the man's children and, hopefully, other relatives too. You may perhaps picture some of them circling like vultures for the pickings. It will inform you of relationships you did not already know of and may well clarify some which you had drawn up only tentatively hitherto. But a will is far more than that simple statement of relationships. It is a personal document. It will tell you much about your ancestor's life-style – whether he was prosperous or poor (poor people made wills too, because their possessions were even more precious to them). It will tell you whether he owned his home or was a tenant; whether he owned or rented other properties, cottages, fields, closes, gardens. It may well tell you what objects he owned as wills often bequeath items of furniture and clothing as well as jewellery and trinkets of all kinds. It may even mention family heirlooms you still own today, but whose origins have become forgotten. It may mention his horse and saddle, his cherished four-poster bed with its drapes, his pigs in the sty, his chickens and chicken hut, his best topcoat and breeches, his best boots (the brown ones he commonly wore on Sundays and his second best pair of black boots he wore for weekdays), his pocket watch, the clock in the hall, which he bought at Derby market for £5.00, and so forth.

Of course some wills are very disappointing, and it might be that he simply left everything to his widow, Winifred. If so you are very unlucky, but you may have better luck with the next one you find. Some wills and, even more, administrations, have an inventory attached to them, which is a detailed list of all his possessions with their current values. These are even more detailed and will mention even the farm tools, the plough, the grindstone, several bushels of wheat, debts owed and owing, the £20 which son John owes him but which debt is now forgiven, the pew he owns in church, his several shares in a copper mine in Cumberland in the parish where he was born. By now you should have an inclination of what potential interest is to be found in a will and, once you reach a certain stage of research, you will be determined to make a thorough search for any and all left by your ancestors.

RECORDING MORE THAN YOU MAY NEED

For the most part we are talking about wills of your male ancestors or their widows or unmarried sisters. Married women very seldom left wills, and when they did it was usually for special reasons – perhaps concerning an inheritance or a dowry they brought with them at marriage. But you will be looking not only for a will for your direct male ancestor, Percival Rollison, whose death you already know was at Catterick in 1797. Searching for that is a simple enough task, since you know the year in advance, and it may be best for you to postpone will searches until you have a few dates of death on record. But when you do carry out a will search, your best plan is to record *every* will and administration in that surname for whatever period you decide to search – a period perhaps twenty-five years each side of a known death date is not a bad idea.

There are several reasons for this. If nothing else, such a list of probates will show you how the surname is spread in that area at that period and this may be very useful if you lose track of the village of origin of your family a generation earlier. Spreading the search date forward to later than the known date of death might just locate a will which for some reason was proved later than usual, that is, of course, if you have failed to find the will at the required date. More important still however is the strong possibility that you may also come across a will for an earlier ancestor, of whose existence you may not yet even be aware. If a will is listed for a Percival Rollison at Catterick in 1744 there is a strong possibility that this person will be related to your Percival dying in 1797, and even if he proved to be an uncle or great uncle, its contents will surely provide you with some useful information.

Before you can search for even a single will you will have had to make the journey yourself, or will have sent an agent, to the appropriate record repository. The cost of the trip is no more if the whole day is spent searching than if only ten minutes is taken to locate one particular will. Personally I would spend the whole day listing all probates as far back and as far forward as time allows. Such a list will give good indication of the scarcity or popularity of the surname in the region, and therefore of the size of the task facing you. But that list will also stand you in good stead for future reference, and as you progress in your pedigree, you will be able to identify certain ancestors here and there, the will of each being already traced.

If you hope to draw up such a list of probates then you would be advised to delay this search until you come to seek a will in the very early 19th, or, better still, the late 18th century. By this date families would tend more often to have been settled in the area for some considerable time, perhaps even as far back as you ultimately trace them. After about 1830 there was much greater mobility of population, especially towards the towns and cities. So if you attempt probate searches *after* your census searches and *after* your initial parish register searches, you will with any luck have already reached a period when your family was relatively static. Once the area is found where a family lived in the late 18th century, they will very often be found always to have lived within maybe a ten-mile or so radius. This applies principally with rural areas, though of course there will be families who are exceptions to this trend.

In searching for wills you are looking first and foremost for male ancestors in your direct line, as these are of the most immediate interest to you. Whether you find the required ones or not, you should also be looking out for the wills of brothers and sisters of your ancestors, which should cause no great difficulty as you will have a list of *all* the probates in that surname in your file. Your direct ancestors may well be mentioned in such wills as being nephews or nieces, or great-nephews/nieces. Best of all, you should always be on the lookout for the wills of spinsters. Maiden aunts had no issue of their own and everything they owned would revert to the family, but they often loved to mention many kinfolk, even if each was left only a few shillings as a token of affection. A spinster dying at an advanced age would remember kinfolk from way back, as well as the most recently born babies, and the will of such a lady can be like treasure trove to a genealogist.

It always pays to examine the wills not only of direct ancestors, and of their brothers and sisters, but also of every person in that surname in the area, even if apparently at this stage unrelated or unrecognised. If the surname is very commonplace, this may be too formidable a task and, if the pedigree is running well anyway, you may feel this is not worthwhile. If need be you could always backtrack to this later, but for the present you may be too keen to press on to bother with such a general search. This is always a trick to have up your sleeve for use later, if and when you get stuck.

At this stage too you may not wish to pursue another line of enquiry with wills, namely to search for wills of sisters (of your direct ancestor) who married. By now you will certainly have come across a few such marriages and you ought to have recorded the baptisms of their children, which of course would carry a quite different surname from your own. You will if you are sensible have searched back and forth a little in the parish registers to pick up such details about these sidelines as were readily available. The time may eventually come, perhaps when you are stuck, when you wish to make a direct search for wills of married sisters' husbands, of their children even, and perhaps too of the husband's parents. In just the same way you will search for, or should consider searching for, wills of the parents of the brides of your direct male ancestors, who too may have been doting grandparents. Similarly you may eventually need to consider searching for wills of brothers and sisters of the bride's parents, especially the maiden aunts amongst them.

If nothing else, the reading of a number of wills of people of the same name as the one you are researching will very rapidly familiarise you with the kind of formalised legal wording of wills and the scripts used in writing them for this period. The sooner you acquire that expertise the better, and the less likelihood there is that you might race back so quickly in time that you have difficulty in reading or understanding such documents as you come across.

Pedigree charts for each will

With every will you read you will need to make extracts of the vital details. You can obviously have a photocopy made for future reference but you need short and succinct extracts listing those features pertinent to forming a pedigree. Even if some of the wills you find are already at this stage quite plainly those of your direct ancestors, you should draw up a tiny family tree constructed from only those details given in each will. If you locate six wills you will draw up six small pedigree charts, each one separate from the other and each using nothing but facts from that will itself. A good idea is to sketch this on the bottom of your extract sheet. This will help you avoid jumping to false conclusions, which is something you are almost certain to do sooner or later anyway. By having each will's own pedigree chart, you can thereafter at a single glance check and cross-check just which facts you drew from which source, and this will often help you spot a flaw in your full pedigree if you have made some sort of error.

Eventually you will find you can use wills like the clues of a crossword. You can work up or down, or from side to side, or in all these directions and can chart the results on your pedigree as you go. At this present stage, however, you have not yet traced your very first will and you are no doubt anxious to get on with that and learn the wider ramifications later. So how do you set about finding your first will?

LOCATING A WILL

From January 1858 a unified and simple system of probate applied throughout England and Wales (for Scotland see page 123). Wills and administrations were proved in local probate registries known as District Probate Registries. Here the original will was filed, a copy was made and sent to the Principal Probate Registry in London, and a further 'registered' copy was made in a bound volume. An additional copy may have been made for the relatives (probably by the solicitor handling the affairs of the deceased). These wills can be traced through indexes in quite a straightforward way. The Principal Probate Registry, now known as the

Principal Registry of the Family Division, is located at Somerset House, Strand, London WC2R 1LP. Indexes to all probates were made on an annual basis and copies were sent to all district registries, though many district registries have now passed their older indexes to local county record offices or libraries (usually indexes over 50 years old). You may therefore find it convenient to use the national indexes locally, and these can also be used to trace the death of an ancestor (who left a probate record of course) more conveniently than the indexes of civil registration of deaths (see page 31).

A booklet *Probate Jurisdictions: where to look for wills* by Jeremy Gibson, published by the Federation of Family History Societies and revised regularly, will tell you where these indexes are located today on a county basis. You will need this booklet anyway to help with the search for *pre*-1858 wills, which is a far more complex affair.

Bound volumes of registered wills which were originally held in the district registries, have often today been passed to the local county record office (with *national* indexes). The original wills have often also been surrendered from the local registries to a branch of the Public Record Office, though not in every instance, so that while the local registries may have shed their older documents and indexes, they will still be accessible via either Somerset House or the local record office. This is especially convenient if, for instance, you happen to live in Yorkshire and wish to trace your ancestors who lived in Devon, as you can search indexes for Devon (and elsewhere of course) in your local Yorkshire record office. Copy wills bound into volumes are usually now known as registered wills, but in the past they were called enrolled wills, and the two terms are interchangeable. Proving pre-1858 wills was very complicated, but if you first understand how a will was made and proved, and – most vitally – *where* it was proved, the complications may seem less daunting. So let us look at the system, and the impatient beginner can take comfort from the fact that even if he has no idea of how the system worked (which courts proved which kinds of wills, where all the complicated administrative boundaries lay, or any of the numerous details of the probate system) – he will still be able to find the required wills anyway. If the wills you need are there, they can assuredly be found.

PROBATE OF WILLS PRE-1858

Very few people fully understand the system of probate as it worked in reality before 1858. There *were* basic rules which operated at the time, though sometimes they changed or were varied at other periods. Often, however, these rules were broken at the time of probate, either deliberately or because they were so complicated that those who administered the system did not always understand them. I have myself sometimes found wills which were not proved in the courts in which they ought to have been, but which, thank heaven, were preserved anyway. So whether or not you understand the system as I shall set it out does not really matter in the end because you are going to search *every* court for probate records of your direct ancestors and perhaps of maiden aunts too. Not every court in the land, of course, but every court which *might* have had jurisdiction over the place of death of your ancestor at the time.

Everything centres on the place of death of your ancestor and the place(s) where he owned property, if any. Often these are one and the same. If Percival Rollison died in Catterick in 1797 and owned his own house in the village and nothing else, then Catterick is the centre of the search. If he owned his house in Catterick and another house perhaps twenty miles away, then his properties may have come within the jurisdiction of two authorities and his will *should* have been proved in the higher authority of the two, although what happened in reality was not always what should have happened. In each instance the senior court claimed responsibility. In each case we begin with the lower, local court and proceed step by step through each higher one to the highest. What were these courts?

Before 1858 wills were proved in ecclesiastical courts, which were organised in a tiered structure beginning with the parish unit and rising to the country as a whole. The tiers were:

> The parish with its vicar or rector (but only parishes which
>   were Peculiars)
> The Rural Deanery controlled by the Rural Dean
> The Archdeaconry controlled by the Archdeacon
> The Diocese controlled by the Bishop
> The Province controlled by the Archbishop

These areas are designated (as they existed before 1858 of course) in the parish register maps (see page 50) and in Gibson's *Probate Jurisdictions* already mentioned.

The principal in proving a will was that it was required to be taken before the local court, that is, the *lowest* court in the hierarchy with powers to prove it.

Certain parishes were known as Peculiars and for probate purposes came outside the jurisdiction of the senior courts. A man who died owning property *solely* within a Peculiar could have his will proved in the local *Peculiar* (parish) *Court*, by his local minister. A Peculiar was the lowest court in the hierarchy. Peculiars are indicated in the parish maps mentioned above.

A Rural Deanery was an area of jurisdiction over a number of parishes. A man who died owning property in one or several parishes *within* that Rural Deanery had his will proved in the *Deanery Court*, and not a lesser one. The option always appears to have been open for an executor to take a will to a *higher* court than the lowest in which he was obliged to prove. At all times there were families who did this, in effect going over the heads of the court of immediate jurisdiction. Quite why this is so is not always apparent. It may have been because they felt that a senior court was a safer place to prove (and preserve) the will.

In his book *Wills and their Whereabouts* Anthony Camp recounts the story of how certain probate records were moved from repository to repository, and on one occasion in the winter of 1748 at least one cart full of probates overturned in transit through the Yorkshire Dales and thousands of wills were lost. Small wonder that certain people, particularly those from wealthier backgrounds with more at stake, may have felt it wiser to go direct to a senior court, especially the most senior court in the land, even though they could have more conveniently proved their wills in a local court.

The next senior court was the *Archdeaconry Court*, and if a man's goods lay in more than one Deanery, his will had to be proved in a court not lower than the Archdeaconry Court, which held jurisdiction over a number of Deaneries (and their parishes of course).

The next court was that of the *Diocese* under the authority of the Bishop. It might be known as a Diocesan Court or Episcopal Court but was often called a *Consistory Court*, and covered several Archdeaconries within the diocese. A *Commissary Court* was the same thing as a Consistory Court under the jurisdiction of a delegate (commissary) appointed by the Bishop but covering a single Archdeaconry. In some areas the *Exchequer Court* was the equivalent of a Consistory Court. In short you should not worry about what the court was called, but search each one for the locality in ascending order.

Property in more than one Diocese involved proving the will in the court of one of the Provinces (under an *Archbishop*), of which there were two. The lower one was that of the Province of York, and wills involving property within more than one Diocese in the northern Province (see maps already mentioned) were proved in the Prerogative Court of York. Those relating to the southern Province, the Province of Canterbury, were proved in the Prerogative Court of Canterbury. Property held in more than one Province involved proving at the higher court, the Prerogative Court of Canterbury. These two senior courts are usually known as the PCY and the PCC respectively. The PCY covered Northumberland, Durham, Cumberland, Westmorland, Lancashire, Yorkshire and Nottinghamshire.

The PCC also had jurisdiction over the probates of those who owned property in England and Wales and died overseas or at sea. At least this was the case in theory, but there are wills proved in the PCY of those dying overseas too.

SEARCHING ALL COURTS OF POSSIBLE APPLICATION

An understanding of the probate court system is of undoubted benefit to the genealogist. However exceptions to rules were often numerous, sometimes inexplicable (or at least inexplicable till *after* the probate record has been found, because you may well not know beforehand what properties the testator owned or where they lay), and could not be anticipated in advance. For this reason the sensible genealogist will ignore the rules and search each court of possible application, one by one, for all probates which might relate to the problem in hand. This may at most involve five or six courts, but until all those applicable have been searched, you cannot be sure that you have failed to trace the required will. Indexes sometimes include more than one court.

From the outbreak of the Civil War (1642) until a few years after the Restoration (1660) most wills were proved in the PCC. Local courts were inoperative, strictly speaking, during the period 1653–1660, but the researcher would check in PCC wills for a little while either side of this period for safety, say 1642–1665. In other words he will cover the local courts for such periods as wills were proved in them during the Interregnum, but will also check the PCC for this period.

Probate records (before 1858 of course) for the PCC are today at the Public Record Office, Chancery Lane, London WC2A 1LR. There are published indexes of those before 1700. The Society of Genealogists has a card index of those between 1750 and 1800. This is in course of publication. So far initial letters up to M are in print and others will follow. For a fee the Society will search in this index, but the unpublished section is not open to public access. For other periods the original PRO calendars/indexes need to be consulted (see Gibson for full details of indexes available).

Probate records for the PCY at the Borthwick Institute of Historical Research, St Anthony's Hall, Peasholme Green, York YO1 2PW. Indexes before 1688 have been published but for later periods the original indexes and calendars need to be used. Gibson again gives full details.

Apart from the probate records of the PCC and PCY, those for most dioceses, the boundaries of which will often conform to the old county boundaries, will be held at the local county record office – with a few exceptions, again listed in Gibson.

Wills for the whole of Wales are at the National Library of Wales, Aberystwyth, Dyfed SY23 3BU. For Scotland see page 125.

The indexes and/or calendars of probate records to each court will be in the same place as the original documents. Indexes to some courts, or parts of courts (usually the earlier periods), have been published, some have been transcribed and most micro-filmed. There may be copies available at other locations within the area apart from the repository holding the probate records themselves. Microfilm copies have been made of all court indexes and these can be seen at the Society of Genealogists' Library (for pre-1858 probates).

There is an alternative method of tracing a will or administration in England and Wales after 1796 and up to 1857, which may be more convenient. During this period (and later) a duty was payable and abstracts of all wills from 1796 to 1811 and copies of wills from

1812 to 1857 were returned to the Estate Duty Office. These Estate Duty Registers are now at the PRO. Before 1812 the indexes are a little awkward to use, but from 1812 they can facilitate the locating of a will *regardless* of which court it was proved in, and of course each indicates the actual court, thereby leading to easy location of the original will. Be warned, however, that not all wills/ administrations were included, as smaller estates were not taxed. These records are known as the Inland Revenue Death Duty Registers. My own feeling is that, as you will almost certainly be searching the indexes to the various courts anyway, there is little to be gained by searching these too, since failure to find a will through them does not mean that no will exists.

11 Wills 2 – How To Understand Them

When the testator died the procedure followed by the executors appears to have been as follows. The will was taken to the appropriate court and, if satisfied that all was in order, the court would pass probate on the will, known as a Probate Act. The court would normally add the official wording or probate at the end of the original will, or perhaps in a book kept specially for the purpose, known as a Probate Act Book – or possibly in both. A copy was then made of the will, and the original was filed by the court and the copy given back to the executors – sometimes the copy was filed and the original returned to the executors. Some courts would copy out the will into a bound volume, and these are known as enrolled wills or register wills.

When you discover a will in a record office today it might be the original will, or the copy made at the time of probate (both being loose documents and normally folded to a convenient size, and perhaps tied round with string or tape). Alternatively it might be the enrolled will appearing, of course, as a page in a manuscript book. If it is the original will, you will see on it the signatures of your ancestor as testator and of the various witnesses, or their marks if they could not write, each in a distinctively different handwriting, perhaps scrawly, perhaps a trembling hand. If it is a copy will or an enrolled will, then the signatures will be copy signatures (not attempting to imitate the originals) and will all be in the same handwriting; this will be quite obvious to you.

Principally you are interested in the contents of the will and you will be pleased to find any of the three possible versions which might be preserved. Sometimes, however, a repository might have a volume of enrolled wills but might *also* have the original will filed separately. In this case you should also look at the original will since it may have other documents with it which will probably not be noted in the enrolled version. An enrolled will is also known as a registered will, because it was copied into a register – or onto a roll of parchment in earlier times. Some wills may have been passed for probate but not 'registered'; it is believed that an extra fee was charged for registration. Some executors were required to sign a bond to declare that they would well and truly execute the will – much depended on the court itself and its usual practice. Such a bond might be in Latin and if so would usually have an English section too, but it might just throw additional details up not found in the will itself.

Some wills also had an inventory with them, that is, a list of the goods of the deceased and their value. These are most interesting items but were more often called for in the case of letters of administration than in the case of a will, again all depending on

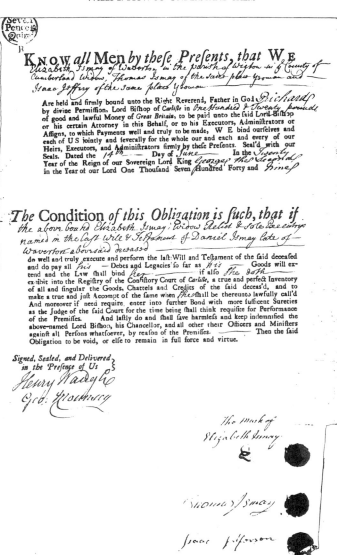

KNOW all Men *by these Presents, that* **WE** Elizabeth Ismay of Waverton in the parish of Wigton in ye County of Cumberland Widow, Thomas Ismay of the said place Yeoman and Isaac Jeffry of the same place Yeoman

Are held and firmly bound unto the Right Reverend, Father in God *Richard* by divine Permission, Lord Bishop of *Carlisle* in *One Hundred & Twenty pounds* of good and lawful Money of *Great Britain*, to be paid unto the said Lord Bishop or his certain Attorney in this Behalf, or to his Executors, Administrators or Assigns, to which Payments well and truly to be made, WE bind ourselves and each of US jointly and severally for the whole our and each and every of our Heirs, Executors, and Administrators firmly by these Presents. Seal'd with our Seals. Dated the *14th* — Day of *June* In the *Twenty* Year of the Reign of our Sovereign Lord King *George the Second* and in the Year of our Lord One Thousand Seven Hundred Forty and *Nine*

The **Condition** *of this Obligation is such, that if* the above bound Elizabeth Ismay Widow Relict & sole Executrx named in the last Will & Testament of Daniel Ismay late of — Waverton aboresaid deceasd

do well and truly execute and perform the last Will and Testament of the said deceased and do pay all *his* — Debts and Legacies so far as *his* — Goods will extend and the Law shall bind *her* — if also *she doth* exhibit into the Registry of the Consistory Court of *Carlisle*, a true and perfect Inventory of all and singular the Goods, Chattels and Credits of the said deceas'd, and to make a true and just Accompt of the same when *she* shall be thereunto lawfully call'd And moreover if need require enter into further Bond with more sufficent Sureties as the Judge of the said Court for the time being shall think requisite for Performance of the Premisses. And lastly do and shall save harmless and keep indemnifed the above-named Lord Bishop, his Chancellor, and all other their Officers and Ministers against all Persons whatsoever, by reason of the Premisses. ——— Then the said Obligation to be void, or else to remain in full force and virtue.

Signed, Sealed, and Delivered,
in the Presence of Us
Henry Wadge
Geo: Mounsey

The Mark of
Elizabeth Ismay
&

Thomas Ismay

Isaac Jefferson

Fig. 11.1 *Testamentary bond to execute will of Daniel Ismay of Waverton and grant probate.*

the court's usual practice. Any such additional papers would be kept with the original will, and these are usually filed in boxes, so it is as well to have a good search through the whole box just in case any papers relevant to your will have become detached and are lying loose in the bottom of the file box.

A WILL, INVENTORY AND TESTAMENTARY BOND OF 1748

Daniel Ismay of Waverton in the parish of Wigton, Cumberland, made his will on 10 August 1748. Filed with the original will is

'a full and perfect inventory of all the goods and chattels belonging to Daniel Ismay of Waverton, deceased, apprised this 7th day of October 1748'.

The inventory includes:

'his horse, purse, apparel and riding furniture, more horses and black cattel, corn and hay, husbandry geir, bedding and bedstead, long settle, table, dresser and other things left by will to Thomas (i.e., Ismay, the son), hemp and line, swine and poultry,'

and in all amounted to £60 15s 0d. On 14 June 1749 probate was granted after the executrix had signed a bond (a testamentary bond) to execute the will, pay any of the testator's just debts, and to exhibit a true inventory of his possessions. The bond is a printed form into which the appropriate names have been inserted, whereby

'Elizabeth Ismay of Waverton in the parish of Wigton in ye county of Cumberland, widow, Thomas Ismay of the same place Yeoman and Isaac Jeffery of the same place Yeoman'

are bound in a bond of £120 to ensure that

'the abovebound Elizabeth Ismay, Widow, Relict and sole Executrix named in the last will & testament of Daniel Ismay late of Waverton abovesaid, deceased'

complies with the conditions. The three signed the bond. Isaac Jeffery is an error for Isaac Jefferson, as Jefferson signed the bond and the inventory with his correct name and witnessed the will itself. Obviously he failed to spot that his name was wrongly written into the bond and must have signed without reading it. These conditions having been compiled with, the Probate Act was then written on a separate sheet:

'At Wigton June 14 1749 on which day appeared personally *Elizabeth Ismay* and alleged that she was and is sole *Executrix*

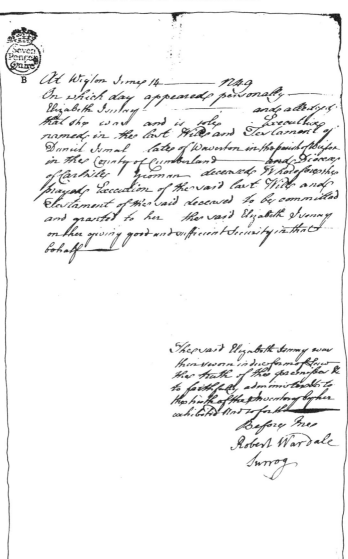

Fig. 11.2 *Probate Act granted to Elizabeth Ismay in June 1749.*

named in the last will and testament of *Daniel Ismay late of Waterton in the parish in the county of Cumberland* and Diocese of Carlisle *Yeoman* deceased wherefore *she* prayed execution of the said last will and testament of the said deceased to be committed and granted to *her* the said *Elizabeth Ismay* on *her* giving good and sufficient Security in that behalf.

'The said Elizabeth Ismay was then sworn in due form of law the truth of the premises & to faithfully administer to the truth of the Inventory by her exhibited and so forth, before me, Robert Wardale Surrog(ate)'

A surrogate was a deputy appointed by the authorities.

While the Probate Act is written by hand it is obvious that a set form of words was used, prepared in advance, and those words set in italics on the original document have been inserted to suit the occasion with space allowed for filling in details as needed.

The testamentary bond is often a printed form into which the appropriate names can be inserted. Sometimes it is in English, sometimes in Latin, and sometimes the first part is in Latin and the second part in English. The English text version of such a bond, and indeed of many other sorts of bonds, commences:

'Know all men by these presents (= these present documents) that we (name of parties here) ... Are held and firmly bound unto the Right Reverend Father in God (name of party here) by divine permission, Lord Bishop of (place here) in (sum of money here) . . . etc.'

The phraseology is legal and boring. All it means is: 'We, the undersigned agree on this date to this bond of £X'. Being bound by such a sum of money (in this case of the Ismay will the sum was £120) did not mean that the bondees had that amount; quite the reverse. This sum was large enough to deter them from noncompliance, and here, as often, it was *twice* the value of the goods in the inventory.

The second part of the bond begins:

'The condition of this obligation is such, that if (name of party) do well and truly execute and perform the last will and testament of the said . . . etc.'

This second part of the bond lists those things the signatory agrees to do; the first part lists the penalties for failing to do them. Many bonds have much the same phraseology, whether they are bonds for marriage, administrations, wills or anything else.

A bond written in Latin was also usually a printed form with spaces for the details to be entered and generally ran: *'Noverint universi per p(re)sentes* . . . ' meaning 'Know all men by these presents ... ' If you cannot read Latin then you will recognise enough to know that it is a bond and you will know its general intent. Certainly you will be able to read the names and other details of the parties involved. The second part, the obligation, is usually in English.

ADMINISTRATIONS AND BONDS

If a person left no will but had possessions of value to leave behind, his next of kin would apply for Letters of Administration. The widow, or other next of kin, would sign an administration bond, much like a testamentary bond. Often in the earlier periods the administrator was required to draw up an inventory of the deceased's goods, though the making of inventories had fallen from custom by the mid-18th century, except in certain special cases. Inventories are usually preserved along with the administration bond. Administrations are generally less helpful to the genealogist than wills, though they will give some detail as to the administrator, and perhaps other relatives too, and certainly an administration is always worth searching for.

Administrations are indexed (or calendared) together with wills in some repositories, and quite separately in others, so you need to be sure to check whether, in looking for your required surnames, you need to search two indexes or one. If time is limited and you have to make a choice, always put a will search first; wills usually contain more genealogical information than administrations.

Another kind of bond found during a search for an administration might be a Curation Bond, which covers guardianship for those under 21 years and probably over 14 for a boy and 12 for a girl. A Tuition Bond covers guardianship of juveniles under Curation age.

When searching for possible wills or administrations you will need to consult indexes of some kind. Those for certain courts have sometimes been published, usually for only certain periods, and often these will be the earlier periods. Some exist in typescript copy form, others may have been microfilmed. For some courts the original documents are accessible only through their own manuscript indexes; other courts may have what are known as calendars. A calendar is a sort of index, usually listing probates in sequence as proved year by year and under the initial letter of the surname. This is not quite as convenient as an index but is the next best thing. You will need to enquire at the record office concerned, as the position is constantly changing as new and improved and more accurate indexes may be drawn up. Reference to J. Gibson's *Wills and Where to Find Them* or Camp's *Wills and their Whereabouts* will indicate the position regarding indexes at the time of publication. So will the more up-to-date *Probate Jurisdictions – Where to Look for Wills* (1989 edition), also by J. Gibson.

19TH CENTURY WILLS

With a will of the 19th century you should have no problem reading the handwriting, nor of understanding any of the content. Towards the latter part of the century the wording is usually something along the lines of this example, which was written in 1898.

> 'This is the last will and testament of me Robert Goode Loomes of Burton on Trent in the county of Stafford retired builder. I appoint my friend William Foxon of Hinckley in the county of Leicester house-furnisher and my wife Eliza Loomes (hereinafter called my trustees) to be the executors and trustees of this my will. I bequeath the use and enjoyment of my watch and chain and my six silver teaspoons silver sugar bowl and two silver table spoons to my said wife Eliza Loomes during her life and after her death I bequeath the same articles as follows the said watch and chain to my nephew Robert Loomes the son of my brother Thomas Loomes absolutely the said silver sugar bowl and two silver table spoons to my sister Emily Ralphs absolutely and the said six silver teaspoons to my sisters Sarah Ann Cross, Fanny Simpson and Martha Foxon absolutely to be divided between them in equal shares . . . '

The will goes on in this fashion. Personal momentos were often shared out in this way so that each relative had something to remember the deceased by, even if they were only objects of small value. Unfortunately sets of items such as the six teaspoons were often split up in this way, which has greatly reduced their value today as antiques, though of course that is only their monetary value.

Already it is very obvious how family relationships can be deduced from a will, and especially one with numerous small bequests. This particular man and his wife died childless, which is no doubt why his will mentions so many kin even in its very early stages, in much the way that the will of a maiden aunt might do. Various other relatives are documented including many of his wife's. My grandfather, then aged 23, got the watch.

My interest at the time was in tracing the direct ancestry of the brother of the tesator, whose 1847 birth I already had traced, and of course I was anxious to press on backwards into historically more interesting periods. At the time I was very inexperienced at genealogy and it would not have occurred to me to work forward over half a century to search for a much later will. By chance a copy of the above will happened to lie among some old family papers, but the information it contained gave so many additional details that it taught me once and for all that in working backwards in time it may often be useful to also consider working forward for wills of side-lines, even though those side-lines may at first seem likely to. be of no more than passing interest.

As I write, I have beside me a will dated 1826, which sets off in just the same manner, that is, in the present-day style of detailing, the testator's name followed directly by his bequests. However, in the 18th century and earlier the opening of many wills began in a somewhat different way. There was no hard and fast time when the introductory style of wills changed as this was a gradual process, just like the change in styles of handwriting. Below is the opening of a will dated 1824, which shows a lingering use of the then old-fashioned opening.

> 'In the name of God Amen I Thomas Looms of the hamlet of Stockingford in the parish of Nuneaton in the county of Warwick farmer being sound in mind memory and understand(ing) being mindful of the uncertainty of this mortal life do make and ordain this my last will and testament in manner and form following that is to say first I recommend my soul to Almighty God that gave it me secondly my body to be buried in my parish church yard at the discretion of my executors and executrix hereinafter named thirdly I will and direct that my just debts and funeral expenses and the expenses of proving this my last will be fully and lawfully paid and from and after the payment thereof I give and bequeath all and singular my household goods and furniture farming stock implements in husbandry and such other personal . . . etc.'

This rambling introduction was typical of many wills, in fact probably the majority of wills made before about 1750. It is quaint but often may seem largely irrelevant to the important details that you want to know of the names and relationships of beneficiaries. It can, however, often contain some very useful clues that you need to look out for. The testator above lived on for a further five years after he made his will. The further back we go the more often do we find that a will was made only when sickness struck and death seemed close at hand. Many turn out to be deathbed wills, and some even left it too late for that. Sometimes people were affected by a sudden and fatal illness and had barely time to gasp out their last wishes to a friend, who either scribbled it down after the man's death or perhaps recounted it verbally to the probate authorities.

Nuncupative will Where no actual will was made but the dying person uttered his last wishes, those who could affirm his last intentions related them to the authorities who would write down and pass probate to what is called a *nuncupative* will, those present at the death being sworn to the truth of his wishes. This was still legally valid, though it has not been since 1837, except in the case of a member of the armed forces dying in action.

OF SOUND MIND

In the preamble to most written wills there was almost always a statement to the effect that the testator was of sound mind, to avoid any question of insanity making the will invalid. Frequently however there would also be a statement about the man's physical state of health – 'being sicke and weake of body' is a typical phrase. Here is a clue that his death is unlikely to be long after, though some made a surprising recovery.

In August 1688 Edmund Appley made his will in Edinburgh, being a watchmaker from Charing Cross, London, 'having come to Scotland about necessary affairs and there falling sick and fearing that my sickness be unto death' – and he was right. Within days, one of the clockmakers he was visiting and a hastily-enrolled executor, Andrew Brown of Edinburgh, paid for the church bells to be rung at his funeral. In September the genuineness of the will was attested to by advocates there and probate was finally passed in the PCC (where his property was, of course) in February following. This example illustrates how a search of the appropriate court(s) can locate a will, even when the testator died in some totally unexpected and distant place.

As well as making affirmations of his faith in God in an attempt to assure his soul a place in the hereafter, many a testator would also make provision for burial and would specify that he was to be buried in the parish churchyard of—, sometimes going so far as to add that he wanted to be alongside his parents or other relatives. The preamble to a will may seem quite charming to you when you first meet it, but after having searched many wills you may feel it to be boring and may be inclined to skip rapidly through it on your way to the (for you) important details. It is usual to make extracts from wills rather than to copy them out in full, and even if you have photocopies made, you would still be well advised to have the briefest extracts set out clearly, line by line, for quick future reference – for you will need to come back to them time and time again in working out your pedigree. By all means extract only the vital details but do not risk missing such clues as explained which can be in the preamble itself.

PROBATE DETAILS – REQUESTS AND BEQUESTS

At the end of the will (or the enrolled will, if an enrolled copy) you will find the probate details. This will tend to be in English on later wills (perhaps after the mid-18th century) but in Latin in most earlier ones. The 1824 will above ends with the mark of the testator and the signatures of the witnesses. You should always record witnesses as well as executors (or 'overseers' as some older wills describe them) as witnesses were often relatives too. The present-day ruling that witnesses cannot be beneficiaries did not apply in the past, at least for all the periods which will concern you.

The probate to the 1824 will reads:

'At Lichfield 5th August 1829. Let a probate of this will be made to Edward Looms the surviving executor named therein, he being first duly sworn and also that the personal estate will not amount in value to the sum of £100. Before me E. S. Remington, Surrt. (= Surrogate) Testator died 20th May last.'

The wording of the probate may vary but the meaning is the same on most wills. Repetitive as it might be, the probate itself can also contain clues. Here for example the actual date of death of the testator is added in the margin, and this is by no means always the case. Also we have another clue in that Edward (who was the testator's son although the probate does not here tell us that) is mentioned as being the *surviving* executor. The other executor (executrix in fact) named in the will was Thomas's wife, Ann, but clearly she had died between the time the will was written and the date of probate. So again you should always read carefully through the probate details and make extracts of the vital items.

Where a testator mentions his children they are often listed in order of seniority, which can also be useful as a clue to locating the baptisms of any hitherto unknown. Normally the sons would be listed first, in order of seniority, and the daughters secondly in the same order. It was usual for children under 21 to be identified as their inheritance would usually be delayed until that age; with daughters it might be 21 or the date of their marriage, whichever was the sooner.

Eventually you are likely to come across the business of one or more children who are left one shilling, and you may well have heard the widely-popular belief that this was the practice of a black sheep of the family being 'cut off with a shilling', in other words an insulting slight. This is quite incorrect. A son out of favour with his father is likely to get no mention at all in the father's will, or perhaps to be offered a bequest if he mends his ways and turns back to the faith or otherwise repents his offending actions. Abel Cottey, a clockmaker from Crediton, Devon, emigrated to Philadelphia in 1682. In his will of 1710 he left his son, John, five shillings 'if ever he returns to this Citty of Philadelphia', and in 1714 Abel's widow stated in her will: 'If my son John Cotty shall come into these parts again I give unto him tenn pounds'. Family feuds may often emerge through bequests.

The practice of leaving one or more children the sum of one shilling each was more a token of affection and would tend to happen in instances where those children had already received such inheritance as they would have had coming. It follows that this will more often apply to the eldest children, who were of age soonest and soonest capable of taking over the family enterprises. The one shilling bequest (or of course any other small sum relative to the testator's wealth) was a courtesy bequest, just so that the affected children did not feel they had been forgotten.

Such small bequests were often also made to friends or others who were to act as trustees, overseers or supervisors of a will. One regular item bequeathed in this way was a mourning ring or a sum of money with which to buy one. Another was a pair of gloves. When Richard France, the Warrington clockmaker, made his will in 1740 he left 'to the clockmakers that come to my burial each a pair of gloves'. Obviously this was a gesture towards his friends in the same trade.

Sometimes the instructions in the preamble concerning the place of burial may contain a clue to nonconformity. When Edward East, the famous clockmaker, made his will in 1688 it contained the unusual sentence 'It is my express wish that my executrix bury me privately in the night time and that she give nothing but Rosemary att my funerall'. Such a request for night-time burial is almost always a sign of nonconformity and it is believed that East may have been a Roman Catholic. The reason for burial during the night was because sometimes funeral processions of nonconformists were targets for drunkards and louts, who might jostle the mourners and jeer at them or even throw stones. During a Quaker funeral in the Yorkshire Dales in the seventeenth century a hostile crowd gathered and jostled the mourners so that the coffin was dropped to the ground and the body rolled out into the street. Burial at night avoided some of these problems. Watch out therefore for any unusual requests and note them carefully as they are unlikely to be just the eccentric preferences of a quirky ancestor, but are real indicators of religious or family custom. Even if your ancestors as far back as you have progressed had always been conformists in religion, you may well find that one member or more turned to non-conformity at some time or other, even if only for a short spell, and such a change of faith could well account for your not having located the expected entries in parish registers.

Before about 1750, wills sometimes had an inventory of the testator's goods attached, a practice which was subject to variation in different regions. Such an inventory may well contain details concerning relatives as well as personal objects that are not in the will. Once you have located a will and examined it, be careful to ensure whether an inventory also exists. If you examine an enrolled will, this is most unlikely to have any inventory with it. You should also therefore check whether the original will itself survives, as these may be kept separately, even if in the same record office. Original wills may have additional paperwork with them, including full details of the probate. But this may be abbreviated, or omitted altogether, in copy wills or enrolled wills. From the original will, you can also verify any possible mis-spelling in the enrolled version. An unusual name, for example, may easily have been mis-copied as it was misread as a more common one – Harker misread as Barker, Timpson as Simpson, etc. Inventories were more often called for in an administration than with a will, but it always pays to ask.

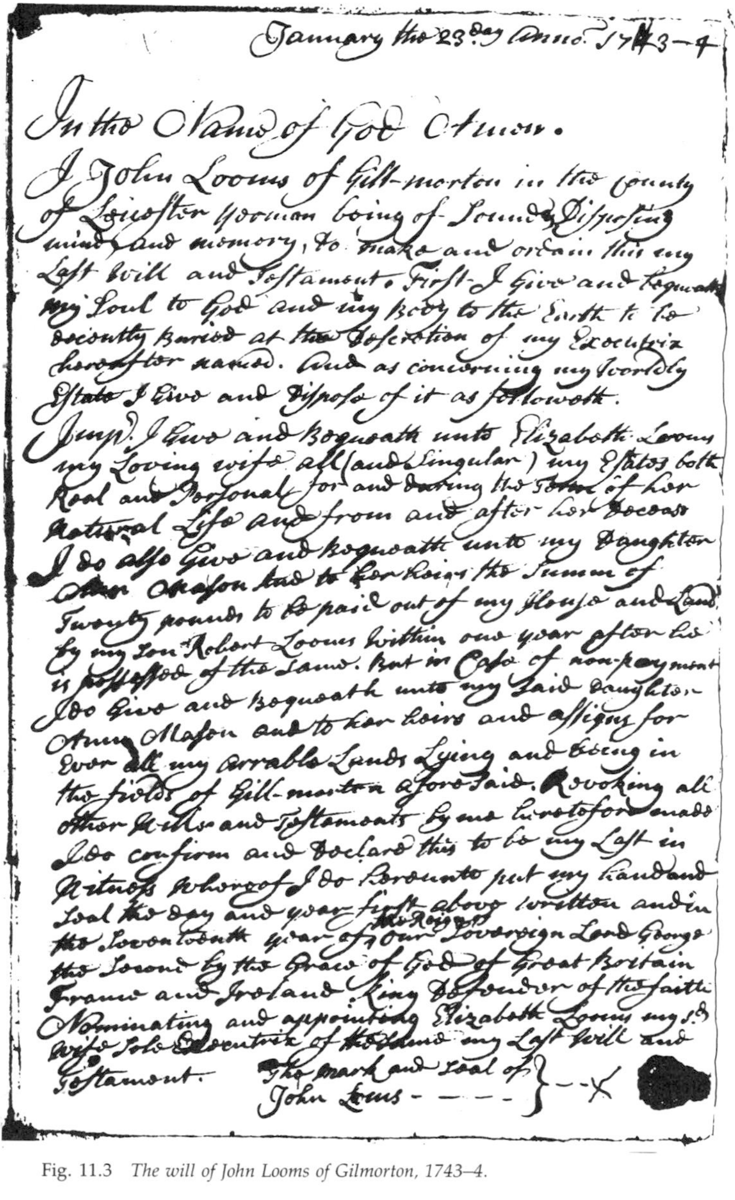

January the 23d day Anno: 1743–4

In the Name of God Amen.

I John Looms of Gilt-morton in the County of Leicester yeoman being of Sound & Disposing mind and memory, do make and ordain this my Last will and Testament. First I Give and bequeath my Soul to God and my body to the Earth to be decently buried at the discretion of my Executrix hereafter named. And as concerning my worldly Estate I Give and dispose of it as followeth.

Imp. I Give and Bequeath unto Elizabeth Looms my Loving wife all (and Singular) my Estates both Real and Personal for and during the term of her Natural Life and from and after her decease I do also Give and bequeath unto my Daughter Ann Mason and to her heirs the Summ of Twenty pounds to be paid out of my House and Land by my Son Robert Looms within one year after he is possessed of the Same: But in Case of non-payment I do Give and bequeath unto my said Daughter Ann Mason and to her heirs and assigns for Ever all my arrable Lands Lying and being in the fields of Gilt-morton aforesaid. Revoking all other Wills and Testaments by me heretofore made I do confirm and declare this to be my Last in Witness whereof I do hereunto put my hand and Seal this day and year first above written and in the Seventeenth year of the Reign of our Sovereign Lord George the Second by the Grace of God of Great Britain France and Ireland King Defender of the faith Nominating and appointing Elizabeth Looms my sd wife Sole Executrix of this and my Last will and Testament. The mark and seal of }—X
John Looms — — — — }

Fig. 11.3 *The will of John Looms of Gilmorton, 1743–4.*

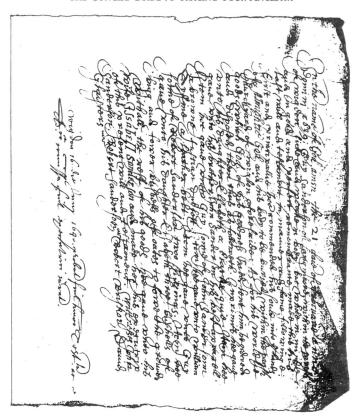

Fig. 11.4   *The will of Guy Sanderson of Wigton, 1639–40.*

The writing in wills and administration documents should not prove much of a problem until the early 18th century, though there were bad and careless writers at all periods. You will need to be on the lookout for eccentric spellings at all periods and also terms for objects long obsolete or forgotten, especially among farming gear and objects of household industry.

Figs. 11.3 and 11.4 are some typical examples and will also serve as reading practice.

Set out in facsimile on page 117 is the will of John Looms of Gilmorton, Leicestershire, written January 23rd 1743–4. The writing is clear enough even in reduced scale.

Fig. 11.4 is the will of Guy Sanderson of Wigton dated 21 February 1639–40, and is transcribed as follows:

> In the name of God, amen, the 21 daie of februarie anno domini 1639; Guy Sanderson of Langmoore within the parish of Wigdon[1], sicke and weake in body, but whole in minde and in good and perfect remembrance made this his last will and testament in manner and forme followinge: First and principallie hee commended his soule into ye hands of Almightie God and his body to be buried within the parish churchyard of Wigdon[1] aforesaid: As for his worldlie goods which God of his goodness hadd sent him he ordered and disposed them thus as followeth. Imprimis hee gave unto his daughter Elsabeth a blacke quie[2]. Item hee gave unto his brother John Sanderson his best apparell. Item hee gave unto Guy sonne of John Sandersonn a browne fustian dublett. Item hee gave unto William Tyffine a leather belt. Item hee gave unto Guy sonne of Robert Sanderson twoo shillings. Item hee gave unto his daughter Elsabeth three bushells of bigg[3] and fower bushells of oates to (?fowr the) ground withall, the rest of his goods hee gave unto his wife Isabell Sanderson and made her his executrix of this present will and testament. Witnesses John Sanderson, Robert Sanderson, Robert Briskoe, David Glaisters.
> Wigdon 16 die Juni 1640 probat. fuit huius testtm. ac Admo. comissa fuit executr(ix?) iurat.

This is clearly a nuncupative will as it is written in the third person expressing what 'hee' wished, rather than 'I' wish. Moreover there is no signature of the testator. This is also obviously a copy will as the 'signatures' of the witnesses are all in the same hand and are copy signatures.

The legal Latin probate details are penned on later in what is clearly a different hand, hurried in style, full of abbreviations and

---

[1] The place is Wigton but clearly written twice as Wigdon.
[2] Quie is the old word for a cow.
[3] Bigg was a kind of wheat.

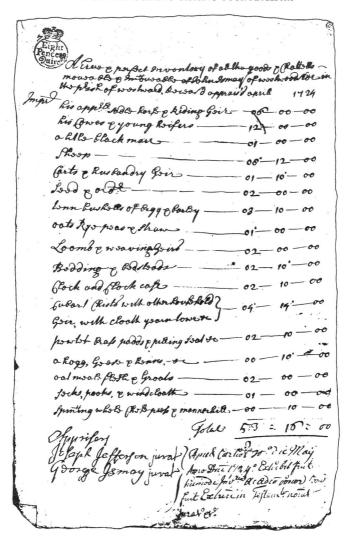

Fig. 11.5 *Inventory of John Ismay, 1724.*

abbreviative flourishes, yet curiously enough still writes Wigton as Wigdon, which was not unusual practice. Perhaps the clerk was copying hurriedly from the document and repeating its spelling. The meaning of the Latin is that probate of the will was granted this day and the executrix was sworn (to faithfully administer).

Here follows the inventory of 1724 of John Ismay of Westward, Cumberland.

A true & perfect inventory of all the goods & chattells moveable & imōuvable of John Ismay of Westwoodside in the p^{r}ish of westward, deceas'd apprais'd april 1724

Impr. his app^{rll}:sadle horse & riding geir	06	00	00
his cowes & young heifers	12	00	00
a litle black mare	01	00	00
sheep	08	12	00
carts & husbandry geir	01	10	00
Seed & (?arde)	02	00	00
tenn bushells of bigg & barley	03	10	00
oats rye peas & straw	01	00	00
Loomb & weaving geirs	02	00	00
Bedding & bedsteads	02	10	00
Clock and clock case	02	10	00
Cubart chists with other household geir, with cloath yearn lowe etc	04	14	00
pewter brass podds & (?pilling seat)	02	10	00
a hogg, geese & henns, etc.	00	10	00
oat meal flesh & groats[1]	02	00	00
secks, ppoks & windcloath[2]	01	00	00
spining whele chese press & mannerhill[2]	00	10	00
Total	53	16	00

Apprisers
Joseph Jefferson jurat   Apud Carliol 30 die Maij
George Ismay jurat   Anno Dni 1724 Exhibit fuit
                          hismodi Inv. ac Adm bonor Com
                          fuit Extricii Testament noiat
                          jurat.

[1] groats – ground oats.
[2] these items unidentified.

12   WALES AND SCOTLAND

WALES – PRINCIPLES AND PROCEDURES

The principles and procedures used in tracing your family tree in Wales are almost the same as in England since, for the preservation of many records, the two countries have been treated as one. Since 1837 civil registration records of birth, marriage and death are kept in the same manner and the same place as those of England, namely at St Catherine's House, Kingsway, London (see page 27). Probate records from 1858 are kept with English ones at Somerset House, London. Those before 1858 for the whole of Wales (including Monmouthshire) are kept at the National Library of Wales, Aberystwyth SY23 3BU, having been proved in local Welsh ecclesiastical courts along the same lines as the English ones. The wills of some Welsh people were originally proved at Chester but these have now been transferred to Aberystwyth, bringing all Welsh wills under one roof.

Wales was within the Province of Canterbury, which was, of course, the senior province, and wills of Welsh people might at any time have been proved in the Prerogative Court of Canterbury (the PCC – see page 103).

Bishops' Transcripts of parish registers, and many original registers themselves are also at the National Library of Wales. Not many have been published, but the Society of Genealogists has transcripts of a number of parishes. To check what exists for individual parishes you need to consult the *National Index of Parish Registers*, volume 13 (Parish Registers of Wales) by C. J. Williams and J. Watts-Williams. The Society also has quite a number of transcripts of monumental inscriptions from Welsh churchyards and chapels.

The Bishop' Transcripts of Welsh parishes have been microfilmed by the Mormons, and these are available at Welsh record offices and Mormon Family History Libraries. These have also been incorporated into the IGI and so are easily accessible, at least the baptisms and marriages should be, as the IGI is weak on burials. The IGI is especially complicated for Wales in view of the patronymic naming tradition there and the question of when the father's Christian name really is the child's surname (see page 93). The use of the Welsh IGI is explained in *Where to Find the International Genealogical Index* by Jeremy Gibson and Michael Walcot (see page 62), as this is rather different from its use elsewhere.

Marriage bonds are at the National Library of Wales, indexed as far as 1837. These have also been microfilmed and should appear in the IGI.

Despite the considerable advances in recent years which have made Welsh records so much more easily available than formerly, the researcher tracing Welsh ancestry has additional problems that are not found in England. One of these is that of the Welsh language, which was in use on official records until recently. It might be that if you have Welsh ancestry you may need to employ a local genealogist familiar with the language. At what point you come up against this language problem will depend on the area and on the records of the parish.

The other problem not found in England is that Welsh surnames became fixed at a much later time than English ones. The system of patronymic naming was especially strong in Wales and persisted into the 17th and even 18th centuries resulting, of course, in an ever-changing surname, which makes tracing impossible. Strong tendency to patronymic naming led to surnames being relatively few in number and hence repetitive. With so many people sharing similar surnames it can be impossible to distinguish one Evan Jones from another. Researchers with Welsh ancestry should read *In Search of Welsh Ancestry* by Gerald Hamilton-Edwards, Phillimore (1986).

SCOTLAND – PRINCIPLES AND PROCEDURES

In Scotland certain records exist for periods different from those in England and Wales, and the nature of many Scottish records is such that, where they exist, they can be more helpful for the genealogist than the English equivalent.

Civil Registration began later in Scotland than in England, namely in 1855 (against 1837). The registration books are kept at the General Register Office, New Register House, Princes Street, Edinburgh EH1 3YT. There you may consult not only the indexes, but the register books themselves, thus enabling you to verify whether or not you have the required certificate entry. Notes can be made of the details, so it is not essential to buy copies of each certificate from which information might be wanted. A microfilm copy of the indexes from 1855 to 1920 is at the Society of Genealogists.

In the first year of registration the information given in certificates of birth, marriage and death was highly detailed, so much so that from 1856 the system was modified to require less detail, and then, in 1861, it was modified again to give a little more. The details of these changes are somewhat complicated but, in general, Scottish certificates give more detail at all times than English ones.

Additional information given in *birth* certificates in Scotland over and above that in England includes: from 1855, age and birthplace of father and mother, when and where married, mother's maiden name, and other issue of the couple; 1856–60, date and place of marriage of parents is omitted; 1861 onwards, date and place of parents' marriage is given again. In *marriage* certificates: from 1855, relationship of couple is given, whether second or subsequent marriage, number of children of any earlier marriage, living or dead, birthplace of each party, name and maiden name of mother of each party; 1856–60, name and maiden name of mother; 1861 onwards, name and maiden name of mother. In *death* certificates: from 1855, place of birth, length of time resident, names and profession of both parents, wife's name if married, names and ages of children, names of parents and of any other of their issue; 1856–60 similar but without place of birth, details of marriage and issue; 1861 onwards, similar.

It is immediately apparent that some of this information will go back a tremendous way in time, over and above that given in England and Wales. So far back does it go that in some cases the informant was unable to give an answer, and sometimes the answers prove incorrect, perhaps from lack of memory.

Also at New Register House are: Marine Registers of Births and Deaths (deaths at sea from 1855 of those of Scottish birth); Service Records (births, deaths and marriages of Scots abroad in military stations since 1881); War Registers (deaths of Scots in the Boer War and World Wars I and II); Births, Marriages and Deaths in Foreign Countries (deaths of Scots abroad since 1860).

Census returns for Scotland are also at New Register House. Microfilm copies of many of them are available locally in Scotland at libraries, where each tend to hold films for their respective areas (usually the old counties). J. Gibson's booklet *Census Returns 1841–81 On Microfilm* will be helpful in establishing who holds what in the way of copies.

Scottish parish registers (the Presbyterian Church of Scotland) are held at New Register House. These are very variable and a good many do not begin before the 18th century. In general they are short in burial information, but for baptisms a bonus is that the name of the mother is usually given. In Scotland it was general practice that a married woman was usually known by her maiden name as well as her married name. The baptism of John the 'son lawful' of Mr Robert Grainger and Mary Peel his spouse is reasonably clear, and would help considerably in a case where you were trying to separate the children of two different Robert Grainger families living at the same time. Less obvious, however, might be a case where the couple were referred to as Mr Robert Grainger and Mrs Mary Peel, as (without the word spouse) you might at first take this to be a child born out of wedlock.

Naming patterns among Scottish children tend to be more rigidly observed than in England, with a regular feature of the eldest son being named after the father's father, the eldest daughter after the mother's mother, the second son after the mother's father, the second daughter after the father's mother. This pattern can also be found in England and Wales but it was a stronger tradition in Scotland.

Some Scottish parish registers appear in the IGI and the coverage is increasing (see *Where to find the International Genealogical Index* by

Jeremy Gibson and Michael Walcot, see page 62).

Wills (in Scotland known as testaments) are held for the period up to 1823 in the Scottish Record Office, Old Register House, Princes Street, Edinburgh EH1 3YY. Indexes for all of these have been published by the Scottish Record Society and will be available in many libraries throughout Britain. After 1823, jurisdiction was under the old Sheriffdoms (more or less the old counties), and some have deposited their wills at the Scottish Record Office, who will advise on their whereabouts and who have indexes to confirmations (the Scottish equivalent to probates). After 1876, a consolidated calendar of confirmations for the whole of Scotland can be consulted there.

Under Scottish law (before 1868) only moveable property (personal property) could be bequeathed by will (known there as testament), and certain proportions had to be left to a man's wife and children if living. The records of testaments outlined above will therefore relate only to personal property. Transfer of land was recorded in what are known as 'Sasines Registers', the principal one being the Old General Register of Sasines (1617–1868), and abstracts of the essential details of these are indexed at Register House at the Scottish Record Office. The Particular Registers of Sasines covers the counties. Both are being indexed, but from 1781 there are indexes to people and places in the abridgements of the sasines, which are easy of access.

To inherit the land of a deceased person the heir had to prove his relationship to a court, and the records of this system are known as the Service of Heirs. These have been published up to 1700 after which date indexes detail the essential information including relationships.

Those researching Scottish ancestors should consult *In Search of Scottish Ancestry* by Gerald Hamilton-Edwards and *Sources of Scottish Genealogy and Family History*, being volume 12 of the *National Index of Parish Registers* published by the Society of Genealogists. A beginner's booklet *Introducing Scottish Genealogical Research* by Donald Whyte is obtainable from the Scottish Genealogy Society Library, 9 Union Street, Edinburgh EH1 3LT. There also exists the Scots Ancestry Research Society, 20 York Place, Edinburgh EH1 3EP.

13 SETTLEMENT

The cost of maintaining the poor of any particular parish fell, at such times that concern us within our research, upon the parish itself by means of such funds as it could raise. The vicar, churchwardens and 'overseers of the poor' were in control of these funds, which were raised by a rate upon the inhabitants as well as certain other sources which might be available. The overseers were local people of some substance and standing. In some parishes the rate books survive and these can be of help in establishing whether an ancestor lived in a certain place at a certain time. Rate books will be in your local County Record Office, if surviving.

The problem facing the overseers of the poor was that those who abused the system might drain the resources to the point where they were insufficient to help the truly needy. There had always been a number of vagrants and beggars – those who drifted from place to place avoiding work though capable of it. The harsh measures brought in to prevent such abuse, from time to time, unfortunately also tended to bear upon those who were too sick or infirm to support themselves. Various procedures were tried with varying success, but fortunately, from our point of view, one particular form of control of the wandering poor began in 1662: the Act of Settlement. This began with the assumption that the upkeep of any parishioner falling upon hard times was the responsibility of the parish of settlement, that is the parish where that person had normally resided in the past, whether born there or not.

THE SETTLEMENT CERTIFICATE
Those who moved from one parish to another were required to bring with them a Settlement Certificate made out by the overseers of the parish of origin and this declared that in the event of that person's falling upon parish charity, the parish of origin would receive back that person and be responsible for his or her maintenance. Settlement within a parish was gained by virtue of length of residence, ability to support oneself, apprenticeship or service. Even workers who moved parish temporarily, such as harvest workers, needed a certificate in order to establish that parish to which they could be sent back if need arose. The overseers were particularly wary of young couples, who might desert their children leaving them in the care of the parish, of unmarried girls who might be pregnant or become pregnant, and of 'lewd women who have bastards'.

The Settlement Certificate itself would have been given to the person concerned to show to the overseers of the new parish as a guarantee against becoming a financial burden, and this was probably kept by its owner and often thrown out when obsolete.

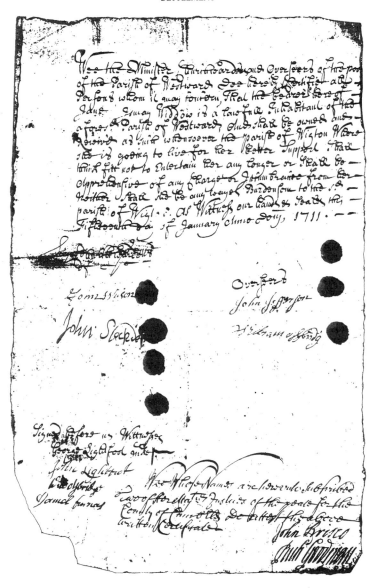

Fig. 13 *Settlement certificate for Jane Ismay, 1711.*

Survival of such certificates would seem then to be a matter of chance but for the fact that the overseers might occasionally have kept a copy or recorded details in some parish ledger. Occasional entries in parish registers will be seen to make reference to those involved as 'strangers' and such reference might well refer to people not settled in the parish rather than the passing strangers they might at first seem to describe. Sometimes the certificate was handed to the officers of the new parish and might have remained with other papers in the parish chest for ever, perhaps long forgotten once the holders had become settled inhabitants.

Settlement Certificates, where they survive, will today be found in the appropriate County Record Office, probably kept on a parish-by-parish basis with any other loose material which has been surrendered. This may, of course, include rate books, churchwardens' accounts, records of the overseers of the poor, and perhaps workhouse records. Workhouses were set up mostly after about 1722 as places where those unable to support themselves might find shelter and work for their keep. Your appropriate record office will know what exists for the parish of your interest.

Fig. 13.1 is a Settlement Certificate as typically set out, though the exact wording might vary from parish to parish. It runs as follows:

Wee the Minister Churchwardens and Overseers of the poor of the Parish of Westward doe hereby certifie all Persons whom it may concern, That the bearer hereof Jane Ismay Widdow is a lawfull Inhabitant of the aforesd Parish of Westward, And shall be owned and Received as such whensoever the parish of Wigton Where she is going to live for her better Support Shall think fitt not to Entertain her any longer or shall be Apprehensive of any Charge or Incumbrance from her neither shall she be any ways Burdensom to the sd. parish of Wigton. As Wittness our hands & sealed this Fifteenth day of January Anno Dom, 1711.

Signed by the Wardens	Overseers
John Wilson	John Jefferson
John Stockdel	William Assbridg

Signed before us Wittnesses	Wee Whose Names are hereunto
George Lightfoot mark	subscribed Two of Her Majts Justi-
John Lightfoot	ces of the peace for the County of
Will Asbridge	Cumberland Do attest the above
Daniel (?)furnas	written Certificate
	John Brisco
	Richd. Goodman

Preserved along with, or perhaps instead of, a Settlement Certificate, might be what is known as a Removal Order or perhaps an Examination Paper. If it came to light that a person had moved into a parish without a Settlement Certificate, or if, without such a certificate, he became a charge on the rates or seemed likely to do so, then a Removal Order might be made out by two Justices of the Peace to direct the churchwardens and overseers to convey (or have conveyed by the constable) this person back to his parish of settlement.

THE EXAMINATION PAPER

An Examination Paper was a document setting out the answers of the 'stranger' to a series of questions posed to determine where his true parish of settlement was. These answers may well give details of age, marital state, number of children, and other personal details, as well as the place of origin and removal, sometimes of birth too. Original Removal Orders or Examination Papers might be preserved in the parish receiving (back) the removed persons, or the parish removing them, or a copy might be with either or both. In some cases of disputed settlement the strangers might have been removed, sent back, removed and sent back again on several occasions before one parish finally accepted liability.

Children born to unmarried women might well become a charge on the parish. Where the father's name was known, it might often be stated in the parish registers, and this was not so much from genealogical interest on the part of the minister, but in order to set down the fact as a statement for future reference. The churchwardens and overseers of the poor would attempt to force the father to maintain the child. This might be done by one of several means including pressurised marriage. One way was to have the father sign a bond (perhaps with others) to agree to maintain the child. If he refused, or denied that the child was his, he might be brought before Justices of the Peace and examined as to the truth of the matter and might be ordered, if deemed responsible, to maintain the child. This could be known as a Bastardy Order and might be attached to or connected with Removal Orders, all of which should be with parish documents. If the father was brought to court then such information would be found through the records of the Quarter Sessions, and other paperwork related to the case would be there. If local Quarter Sessions records are not deposited in your record office, the archivist there will know their whereabouts.

Of all the Settlement Certificates issued only a fraction will survive today, so if your ancestor arrived in a parish from parts unknown, do not assume that you will simply be able to look up the appropriate surviving certificate. Chris Pickford, Bedfordshire County Archivist, estimates the survival rate as being less than ten per cent of those issued. Nevertheless this is one way in which you might be able to trace the parish of origin of an ancestor and it is well worth enquiring into the possibility of such records having survived for your parish of interest. Even if you already know your ancestor's parish of origin before he moved into the parish of later residence, any surviving settlement papers might well give considerable detail you would not find in parish registers. So a search after these may be very rewarding even if you already know the track to follow further back in time. You might even find that your local record office has an indexed list of all such papers held, so do ask the archivist.

For example, if your ancestors happen to have lived in Bedfordshire you are particularly fortunate in this respect as Bedfordshire Family History Society in association with Bedfordshire County Record Office has just published an index by surname and parish of all surviving poor law papers in the county. These include apprenticeships (by the parish), Bastardy Papers, boarding out of infants, Examination Papers, Indemnity Bonds, militia references, Removal Orders, and any other poor law papers. Few Record Offices will have such easily accessible settlement archives, but it always pays to enquire.

The whole business of settlement is more complicated than this brief résumé. More detail will be found in *The Parish Chest* by W. E. Tate (CUP 1985), and this is certainly the book to consult if you should trace settlement papers which are not immediately understandable. For more information on Quarter Sessions records see J. S. W. Gibson's publication *Quarter Sessions Records for Family Historians: A Select List* (Federation of Family History Societies).

Below is the text of an Examination Paper and its related Removal Order, published by permission of Bedfordshire County Record Office, Eaton Socon Parish Records. The finding of one such document about an ancestor would be a stroke of luck. Finding two together about the same person is extremely unusual.

Bedfordshire. to wit. The Examination of Eden Wadsworth Clocksmith and Watchmaker touching the place of his last legal settlement

This Examinate on his oath saith That he was born at Great Barford in the County of Bedford where his Father William Wadsworth lived and rented a small Farm – That his Father afterwards removed to Thurleigh in the said County of Bedford and hired a Farm there of more than fifty Pounds per annum and this Examinate went and lived with him as part of the family – That at about the age of fourteen he was with the consent of his then father in law Sam Eden bound Apprentice to Mr. William Peck of Bolnhurst in the said County of Bedford Clocksmith and Watchmaker for seven years from the twenty seventh day of April one thousand seven hundred and seventy eight and served under the said Indenture four years or rather more In which time his Master removed to Keysoe in the said County of Bedford but continued to carry on the business of a Watchmaker at Bolnhurst aforesaid and this Examinate worked and slept at Bolnhurst aforesaid till within about ten or fifteen days of his leaving his said Master when he went to Keysoe and slept there – But previous to his removal to Keysoe his master desired him to pack up all his papers for him which he this Examinate did and amongst the Papers found both parts of the Indenture of Apprenticeship between him and his master which he concealed from his master – That he left his Master without his concurrence and endeavoured to obtain (employment) from Mr. Cavit of Bedford watchmaker who refused taking him until he had been properly discharged from his apprenticeship – and thereupon his then father in law Edward Wildman of Ravensden in the said County of Bedford agreed with the s^{d} William Peck for this Examinat's discharge for one Guinea which was paid to Peck by said Wildman and he this Examinate then left his said Master – Then worked (with^{d}) at his business at Mr. Cavit's and in various other places sometimes by the week and sometimes by the Great [sic] – Then entered into the Marines and was discharged therefrom (being in the forty ninth Company or division) at Chatham the eleventh day of April One thousand eight hundred – Since which he has only worked by the week or Great and never for a year and hath done no act since to gain himself a legal Settlement elsewhere – That he was married at Ravensden in the said County of Bedford and hath a Wife now living named Sarah and two Children born in wedlock Elizabeth aged (seven^{d}) eight years and upwards and Eden Wadsworth (a boy) aged (three^{d}) four years and upwards.

Sworn before us this
ninth day of October 1813   Eden Wadsworth
   Robert Moore
   Hugh Wade Gery

Those items marked 'd' have been deleted in the document.

To the Church-Wardens and Overseers of the Poor of the Parish of Eaton Socon *in the* County of Bedford *and to the Church-Wardens and Overseers of the Poor of the* Parish of Bolnhurst in the said County of Bedford

WHEREAS Complaint hath been made unto us, two of his Majesty's Justices of the Peace acting in and for the County of <u>Bedford</u> aforesaid (one whereof being of the Quorum,) by the Church-Wardens and Overseers of the Poor of the said <u>Parish of Eaton Socon That Eden Wadsworth and Sarah his Wife, Elizabeth their Daughter aged eight years, and Eden their Son aged four years have</u> lately intruded, and came into the said <u>Parish of Eaton Socon</u> and <u>are</u> become chargeable to the same; we and the said Justices, upon Examination of the Premises upon Oath, and other Circumstances, do adjudge the same to be true, and do also adjudge the Place of the last

legal Settlement of the said <u>Eden Wadsworth, Sarah his Wife</u>
<u>& Elizabeth & Eden their Children to be in the said Parish of</u>
<u>Bolnhurst, in the said County of Bedford</u>

THESE are therefore in his Majesty's Name, to require you,
the said Church-Wardens and Overseers of the Poor of the
said <u>Parish of Eaton Socon</u> on Sight hereof, to remove and
convey the said <u>Eden Wadsworth, Sarah his Wife and</u>
<u>Elizabeth & Eden their children</u> from and out of your said
<u>Parish of Eaton Socon</u> to the said <u>Parish of Bolnhurst</u> and
<u>them</u> deliver unto the Church-Wardens and Overseers of the
Poor there, or to some or one of them, together with this our
Order, or a true Copy hereof, who are hereby required to
receive and provide for <u>them</u> according to Law. Given under
our Hands and Seal this <u>ninth</u> Day of <u>October 1813</u>

<u>Bedfordshire</u>   <u>Robert Moore</u> [seal]
                                                 <u>Hugh Wade Gery</u> [seal]

This Removal Order is a printed document with the underlined
sections entered in manuscript. The information given in the
Examination Paper is unusually detailed and includes some items
of the man's life that might never been discovered through any
other source.

14   RECORDS OF APPRENTICESHIP

If your ancestor was a craftsman he may well have served an apprenticeship to learn his trade, and if you can locate a record of this, not only will it tell you more about the details of his life, but it will almost certainly specify his parentage and place of origin. Not all craftsmen served an apprenticeship, even though they may have undergone just as long a period of training. In the case of a son learning his father's trade, for instance, there may have been no formal apprenticeship, no paperwork, no records. Some sons *were* formally apprenticed to their fathers and this may have been the more likely in a large city such as London, where the apprentice may have been required to produce written proof of his training in the recognised manner before being allowed to practise his craft there. In the cities the control of the trade guilds was very strong. In the countryside the trade guilds had no control and craftsmen, trained or otherwise, could set up as they felt inclined.

APPRENTICESHIP PROCEDURES
A legal contract, known as an indenture, was drawn up and signed by the apprentice on the one hand and the master on the other. The indenture specified the terms of service, which varied a little in different parts of the country although most contained very similar provisions. The indenture itself would have been kept by the apprentice, so these survive only by chance, though the pertinent details may have been preserved or documented, as we shall see. A youth was normally bound at the age of fourteen to serve for seven years and thus be free of service when he was of full age, that is twenty-one. Occasionally, and principally in the period before about 1650, an apprentice may have been taken at an earlier age, exceptionally as young as ten, and would therefore be likely to serve a longer period until he was twenty-one. In some trades he may then have had to work under his own master, or another, as what was known as a 'journeyman' for up to two years before being permitted by the guild to set up on his own account.

Completion of apprenticeship was recognised by most guilds by means of a process known as taking up 'freedom' in the guild, which meant freedom from apprenticeship and freedom to practise the craft. Freedom in some cities, probably most, was essential as the guilds were jealous of too much competition for existing traders, and they would prosecute non-freemen who sought to trade there. Those cities which had the apprenticeship system controlled by a guild or the corporation, or both, will usually have records preserved in good order detailing names of apprentices and masters, dates of freedom, and perhaps other information too. Your local County Record Office will know what records exist for the towns within your county of interest.

There was no centralised recording of apprenticeships as such and these records, if they exist at all, will be kept on a town by town basis. There was however a centralised system of recording tax paid on apprenticeships, which is the next best thing, and this is explained later.

FREEDOM TO TRADE

Freedom to trade in the larger towns and cities was granted in other ways as well as through apprenticeship, though procedures may have varied from town to town. Sons might inherit the right to trade by virtue of the father's existing right, usually noted in the records as being by patrimony. Others might be able to purchase the right to trade by payment of a fee, known as freedom by redemption, though such applicants may have to produce evidence of apprenticeship to show that they were qualified to the required standards. Freedom resulting from apprenticeship was known as freedom by servitude.

It should be remembered that even a rural craftsman might have decided to take up freedom in a town some distance away from his place of trade if, for instance, he wanted the right to trade there at certain times, such as market days. Examples do exist in some city freedom records of craftsmen who worked perhaps 20 or 30 miles away, so freedom in a certain town should not be regarded necessarily as evidence that the man lived in that town.

London was a special case for numerous guilds existed there. They were known as City Companies, and each would cover a certain trade or group of trades. Craftsmen wishing to trade in London would probably first have to satisfy a City Company of their competence and obtain freedom in that company. The same routes to freedom were open to them there as in other cities, namely servitude, patrimony and redemption. But the trade followed by a particular craftsman may not necessarily have been that of the company in which he obtained his freedom. This probably arose from the method of entry by patrimony, whereby the son of, say, a clockmaker may have followed a different trade from his father yet may still have had right to freedom in the Clockmakers' Company by patrimony, even if his trade was in no way connected with clockmaking. In checking on freedom of a particular ancestor in London, you may therefore have to search the (often indexed) records of numerous City Companies.

To trade in London, however, it often involved not only freedom in a particular City Company but also freedom of the City itself, and these City freedoms were controlled by the Chamberlain. Often a man was free in a City Company first, followed by freedom of the City; sometimes he was free in the former and not the latter; sometimes vice versa. Different procedures seem to have been applied at different periods, and perhaps for reasons not apparent to us. For instance a craftsman who wished to practise by working under another master (i.e., as a journeyman) might have been allowed to do so by virtue of his Company freedom and may not have needed City Freedom, which one wishing to open his own trading shop would have needed. Conversely, I know of examples where a craftsman was refused freedom by a City Company but was granted City freedom, thus forcing the City Company to accept him (or some *other* City Company perhaps). A tradesman who was a freeman of a City Company and of the City of London would style himself in records as e.g., Henry Jeeves, Citizen and Haberdasher. This does not simply mean that he lived in London, but that he was free of the City. Nor does it necessarily mean that he was a haberdasher by trade, though he may have been.

The records of freedom of the City of London are at the office of the City Chamberlain, Gresham Street, London. Records of many City Companies (though not all of them) are at the Guildhall Library, Aldermanbury, London. Some have been published; others are well indexed. Some City Companies still retain their records and in such cases you would need to apply to the Clerk of the Company in question. The Guildhall Library will know the whereabouts of Company records not yet deposited there. If you do not know whether your ancestor was a Company or City freeman your simplest step is to search the City Freedoms first, because the individual Company records will need to be searched one Company at a time, and there are many of them and not all have records easy of access.

Before you attempt to search for a Company freedom (that means only *London* City Companies of course) or a freedom of the City of London, it may be more profitable to search for a record of an apprenticeship by means of the tax records described below. Incidentally, the Companies of the City of London controlled the trade essentially only in the capital itself within something like a ten-mile radius. They had no jurisdiction in the provinces, though they sometimes sought it. Occasionally a provincial tradesman was admitted to freedom in a London City Company, though these instances are infrequent and probably more by way of an honour than an obligation. Those who sought to trade in London were forced into joining a Company or were hounded by prosecution that aimed to prevent them trading there, though some traders persistently refused to join Companies and seem to have got away with it.

TAX ON INDENTURES

From 1710 to 1810 a tax was placed on indentures and records of such taxes are preserved at the Public Record Office, though they are not indexed. However the Society of Genealogists has an index for the period 1710–1774, a copy of which is at the Guildhall Library. From 1774 to 1810 the un-indexed originals have to be used. The index is to both apprentices and masters. The indexes cover the British Isles and include apprentices through London

City Companies. They show name of apprentice, his father, place of origin, length of service, amount of the premium paid and the tax payable (by the master). The premium was the sum paid by the parent to the master and would vary from as little as £2 to over £50 on occasion. They also show the trade of the master and of the boy's father. Girls were sometimes apprenticed too but here the trade shown as that of the master was rarely that followed by the girl. A girl was usually 'apprenticed' to serve the master's wife in a domestic capacity, though sometimes to follow the wife's trade such as a milliner. You can take it that a girl apprenticed to a blacksmith was not going to wield hammers!

About half way through these indexes the father's name ceases to be given. Remember that details of some of these apprenticeships may *also* be recorded in local records of those towns (York, for instance) which kept records of freedom, so that additional information might be available in the locality once you have found from these centralised indexes that an apprenticeship existed. Remember too that, like all indexes, these are fallible.

These records originated as a centralised method of checking that tax had been paid. They were made out by the Office of Inland Revenue from returns submitted by local collectors, who submitted summaries from sub-collectors. In consulting these indexes you are working from an index of a copy of a copy of a copy! Not surprisingly they contain errors, and, knowing the compilers, these are not likely to be in the tax amounts but in the names and localities. A little ingenuity may be needed to gain maximum benefit from them. The following example illustrates just what can happen.

I was trying to investigate the background of clockmaker, John Ismay, who was known to have worked at Wigton, Cumberland, in the second quarter of the 18th century. Ismay was one of a small group of clockmakers there whose work was eccentric enough to reveal what I thought were signs of influence of another clockmaker, John Ogden of Askrigg, Yorkshire. The index was searched for John Ismay with no success, but under John Ogden (several of whose apprentices were already known to me anyway) the following entry was found: 1711. Wray, Jn (son of Leonard) of Thursby, Yks, yeo. to John Ogden of Bowbrigg Hall, clock. £10.

I knew this was *the* John Ogden, though the address was unusually scant, giving only the name of his house and not even the county. What was most puzzling was that no clockmaker named John Wray had previously been recorded (ascertained by checking several dictionaries of clockmakers which are reasonably comprehensive). Of course not all apprentices finished their term – some died and some absconded and some decided not to follow that trade after all, so that the evidence of an apprenticeship by no means always indicates that the person took up that trade afterwards.

However the village of Thursby is not in Yorkshire, as the index states, but in Cumberland and is immediately adjacent to Wigton. Armed with this clue I searched Thursby parish registers for John Wray, but found the name Wray did not occur at all nor any spelling variants of it. I did find a number of Ismays, including a John who would fit my original bill, but no son of Leonard – in fact Leonard is a very uncommon first name anywhere at this period. By now I suspected that the index had misread Ismay as Wray, understandable if the letters were of a flourishing nature. But Leonard was really puzzling. I wrote to the Public Record Office for copies of any original entries. This, by the way, is not to be recommended as the information is little more than the indexed abbreviation and such copies are very costly. Normally there would be no point in paying for this, but here was a special case. The result was:

> Sep 4th 1711 John Ogden of Bowbrigg Hall in Com. York, Clockmaker – John son of Leonard Wray of Thursby in Com. York, Yeom. (to run) 7 years from 26th June, Common Indenture, Elizabeth Hall at York, £10. 5s.

The abbreviation Com. is short for Latin *in comitatu* = in the county of. Elizabeth Hall of York was the collector (or sub-collector). £10 was the premium and 5 shillings the tax paid.

So the index had copied the names faithfully, but the names Wray and Leonard were still incorrect. Eventually I worked out that the return itself must have been carelessly written. Wray had been misread for what was Ismay. Leon(ard) had been misread from what was no doubt John, again probably badly written (Leo. as Jno?). This was a very special case and if I had simply been tracing the ancestry of John Ismay, I would never have found this apprenticeship, as I could hardly have known his master's name in advance. My cross-checking against John Ogden was purely intuitive based on the fact that I knew something of his work – a long-shot happy deduction which can sometimes come one's way.

Incidentally there appears on the same page of the index an example of a girl apprentice:

> 1711. Hannah Baines daughter of Ann Brown of Kelfield in Com. York to John Bywater of the city of York, Semstris & laundresse.

John Bywater could hardly have been a female launderer, and evidently it was his wife who was to train the girl, though the indenture was made out in her husband's name as master. An intriguing genealogical problem is posed in that the mother of Hannah Baines has the surname Brown, which as we already know might be for one of several reasons.

There were two kinds of apprenticeships which were not subject to the tax: those where the premium was a nominal amount, as might be the case if a father took his own son as apprentice; and those where a child in the care of the parish, or perhaps of poor parents, would be put to apprenticeship by the parish (i.e., at parish expense), where again the premium was likely to be small or nil. Records of such apprenticeships, if they survive at all, might be jotted in the parish registers or churchwardens' accounts or other parish papers. Or perhaps occasional indentures may have come into the hands of your local County Record Office, which is the place to enquire for stray apprenticeships, as well, of course, as checking such records for the larger towns in your area. The Society of Genealogists has a miscellaneous collection of about a thousand original indentures.

AN ORIGINAL INDENTURE

Below is the wording of an original indenture surviving amongst the records of the Worshipful Company of Clockmakers, London.

> This indenture witnesseth that Richard Allen son of John Allen of Pangbourne in the county of Berks, Gent:-------------- doth put himself apprentice to Henry Harper, Citizen and Clockmaker of London, to learn his art: and with him (after the manner of an apprentice) to serve from the day of the date hereof:------------------------------ unto the full end and term of seaven years, from thence next following to be fully compleat and ended. During which term the said apprentice his said Master faithfully shall serve, his Secrets keep, his lawful commandments every where gladly do. He shall do no damage to his said Master, nor see to be done of others but that he to his power shall lett or forthwith give warning to his said Master of the same. He shall not waste the goods of his said Master, nor lend them unlawfully to any: He shall not commit fornication nor contract matrimony within the said term. He shall not play at cards, dice, tables, or any other unlawful games, whereby his said Master may have any loss. With his own goods or others during the said term without licence of his said Master he shall neither buy or sell. He shall not haunt taverns or play-houses, nor absent himself from his said Master's service day or night unlaw-fully. But in all things as a faithful apprentice he shall behave him self towards his said Master and all his during the said term. And the said Master his said apprentice in the same art which he useth, by the best means that he can, shall teach and instruct, or cause to be taught and instructed, finding to his said apprentice, meat, drink, apparel, lodging, and all other necessaries, according to the custom of the City of London during the said term. And for the true performance of all and every the said covenants and agreements either of the said parties bindeth himself unto the other by these presents. In witness whereof the parties abovenamed to

these indentures interchangeably have put their hands and
seals the eighteenth day of August in the eighth year of the
reign of our Sovereign Lord King William the Third of
England, etc. Anno Dm. 1696

      Francis Speidell.   Richard Allen.

Francis Speidell was Clerk to the Company, and has evidently
signed in place of the master. This is very unusual and it may be
a duplicate indenture made out for the Company's own files,
hence not signed by Harper.

15   MONUMENTAL INSCRIPTIONS,
NEWSPAPERS, DIRECTORIES

If you can locate a monumental inscription for your ancestor it may contain all manner of information not otherwise available. One bonus may well be that a grave will contain several different members of a family, and the tombstone will probably explain the relationship, perhaps offering clues that might not be available elsewhere. So, sooner or later you ought to be searching for tombstones of your ancestors, or at least the details from them, for many graves may today have been removed for developmental reasons and the stones themselves no longer exist.

Just at what point in your research you tackle this aspect will depend on the circumstances of your family tree as you begin to unfold it. I shall never forget, many years ago, getting into my car, driving two hundred miles to a village where I knew my ancestors had lived in the mid-19th century, strolling into the churchyard and within minutes finding several tombstones which offered a mass of detail not only about the ancestors I was aware of, but others too who were quite new to me. This was an amazing piece of luck, although at the time I didn't fully realise it. There is nothing to stop you doing the same thing, but it could waste your time and it is not recommended practice.

CHURCHYARD TOMBSTONES AND TRANSCRIPTS
In many churchyards you will find the tombstones overgrown, fallen face down into the earth, weathered away to the point of illegibility, or piled up in heaps in a corner due to road widening. Add to this the problem that some graveyards contain hundreds of graves and such a search might take days and still prove inconclusive. Was your ancestor's grave not there after all (death certificates do not state the place of burial)? Or was it one you were unable to read? Had the stone been removed, or was there perhaps never a tombstone at all? Not all graves had a stone memorial: among certain groups of Quakers, for example, a tombstone was regarded as a sign of vanity and was not permitted.

Some Quakers did raise tombstones, often in such a way that each stone was the same as its neighbour in order to ensure equality. On one occasion I discovered, in the course of researching a Quaker family, that meetings had been held in the house of one of them and burials had taken place in the garden, although this particular site was not recorded as a known Quaker burial ground. I visited the site hoping to discover some long-forgotten tombstones only to find that the house had been levelled some years ago and a modern bungalow now stood in its place. The present occupiers had no knowledge of any tombstones and it is supposed that any that might have been there had been bulldozed clear and perhaps used in the foundations.

It is because of the transitory nature of even these stone monuments, which were intended to be permanent markers, that some enthusiasts have transcribed details from them to form a more permanent record. The work continues today among a small group of the dedicated, and often local history groups will try to record tombstones before it is too late.

Monumental inscriptions (often known as MIs) may be published as books, typed and indexed, or written in manuscript form. Your first step should be to try to establish whether any transcribed MIs exist for the parish of your interest, as it is far quicker and more satisfactory to consult such a transcript if it does exist. You may of course be unlucky, but a check is always worthwhile, as you might find that a nearby parish has also been copied and you could find an unexpected grave of a close relative.

If you have been able to trace your ancestry to a small country parish then it may well be feasible for you to make a personal visit and try a search of the gravestones, if you are quite certain that no transcript exists.

Your local County Record Office is likely to know what transcriptions exist of local tombstones and, of course, church brasses too, which would be included in any such transcript. If the county of interest has a local history society, or antiquarian or archaeological society, they too should know of such transcripts and may well be engaged in recording them themselves. Such a society almost always has one keen devotee of the subject and he is sure to have a detailed knowledge of what exists and where to find it.

The Society of Genealogists has a large collection of MIs; it also has a booklet listing all those that are known.

TOWN AND CITY CEMETERIES, POST-1853

Following an Act of Parliament of 1853 many towns and cities opened their own cemeteries. Well-kept records often exist of these more modern burial places, and of course a city might have several different ones. The town clerk of the local council will know the whereabouts of such records or will direct you to a source that will know, but it may not be practical for a search to be made in a number of cemeteries in a particular city. It may therefore be best if you delay attempting your search until you have some strong clues as to the district in which your ancestors lived and, ideally, the address, as this may indicate the cemetery records lying closest at hand.

NONCONFORMIST BURIALS

Nonconformists either had their own burial grounds or were buried in the parish churchyard. This would vary at different periods, sometimes depending on their own inclination, sometimes on the consent of the vicar. Nonconformists were often buried in a particular part of the churchyard, or even a small plot of land adjacent to it but outside the consecrated ground. If your ancestors were nonconformists then they will often be recorded in their own registers of death, in which case the place of burial might well be named.

TRANSCRIPTS, PRESS NOTICES AND DIRECTORIES

The Federation of Family History Societies is engaged in a massive campaign through its member societies of recording all inscriptions from churchyards and burial grounds, and tremendous progress has been made during these last few years. The local Family History Society from your area of interest will know what transcripts exist. These are an immense benefit to researchers and open up an avenue of inquiry which previously was only available to those willing to treck to the churchyard in person and scramble through the undergrowth, pencil in hand.

Obituaries were of course published regularly in newspapers and while we might think of these principally in relation to people of fame, or at least some local standing, there were also notices of death entered by the family, and for that matter of weddings and births too. A report of a funeral in a local paper might well mention a list of mourners, including relatives.

Some newspapers extend back well into the 18th century, a fact which often comes as a surprise to a beginner. Early ones are often indexed and the record office of your family's 'home' county may have such an indexed series. Often such indexes will refer not only to news items but to advertisements of tradesmen and if your ancestor was in any one of the dozens of trades seeking their customers from the public at large, you might well find some helpful notice about him. When such a tradesman first set up shop in a new town or village he would often advertise the fact in the county newspaper of the day, and frequently he would specify his place of origin and the names of the people he had worked for or trained under. A death notice can often supply unexpected detail.

In 1780 the 'Leeds Mercury' announced:

'Died suddenly after eating a hearty dinner, Mr. Henry Gamble, an eminent clockmaker, near Pudsey'.

An example of this kind of extraordinary background detail also appears in the 'Ipswich Journal' of December 1773:

'Nathaniel Cavell, clock and watch maker, formerly apprentice to Mr. John Page of Ipswich (and lately come from London) has moved from his shop near the Great White Horse and has taken the shop and stock late the said Mr. Page's in the Butter Market.'

The British Library Newspaper Library, Colindale Avenue, London NW9 5HE has a large collection. For provincial newspapers and journals at least one library within the county will have copies and you may well find with the older ones that extracts have been published by a local history society. A publication by J. S. W. Gibson, *Local Newspapers 1750–1920* (Federation of Family History Societies), will tell you what exists.

In locating an ancestor who was a tradesman the older trades directories can be of help. Some exist from the mid-18th century but on a random basis varying by county, as it was not until the second quarter of the 19th century that regular series of directories were published.

Some directories, principally the later ones after about 1850 will list private citizens. Before that they are really only useful for picking up tradesmen and business people; the private individuals in the earlier directories (pre-1850) tend to be people of substance.

If your ancestor was a craftman who signed his goods, then you should also consult present-day reference books on those crafts. There are many good biographical dictionaries of such trades as gunsmiths, jewellers, goldsmiths, silversmiths, pewterers, cabinet-makers, clockmakers, artists. Not only might such works contain information about your ancestor but if you read something of the craft itself, this may lead you towards trading centres of that craft, which could help you establish routes of possible migration for a moving ancestor.

16   HERALDRY

Most people have a vague idea that heraldry involves coats of arms and crests, but know little else about this very specialised, complicated subject. I shall hope to explain a little of it, but your prime interest in heraldry when tracing your family tree is in the answers to the following questions. First, does my family have a coat of arms and, if so, how can I find out what it is? The answer is probably in the negative, but you don't have to take my word for it; you can find out for yourself. Second, does my family have a crest? The answer is the same. A crest is part of a full coat of arms and cannot exist apart from it (though it might be seen separately, for instance, on a dinner service). The third question is: will a knowledge of heraldry help me in tracing my family tree? Again the answer is, probably not, but the truth is we are all intrigued by the idea of heraldry, and surely heraldry and genealogy are closely connected?

Before we answer that, let us ask another question: what about the advertisements often seen offering to 'look up' your coat of arms for you and even to supply you with a colourful copy of it on a small shield to hang on your sitting room wall? Well, what those people who sell painted shields for the wall will do for you, for a fee naturally, is to look in a book known as an 'armorial' (of which there are many), check whether a coat of arms exists in your surname, select one of the several they might find in that name and paint it neatly for you. You can, in fact, look up your name for yourself in any library if you wish. If your name is Robinson, you will probably find half a dozen coats of arms or more, and they may truly be coats of arms in your surname, but none of them is *your* family coat of arms.

WHAT IS A COAT OF ARMS?
A coat of arms belongs to the family to whom it was granted, and to male heirs of that family. It certainly does not belong to other people who happen to have the same surname, and who feel like using it. To adopt a coat of arms which by right belongs to someone else is illegal, though it is unlikely anyone is going to take action against you for hanging a Robinson coat of arms on your wall. Of course if you are able to prove your descent from someone who correctly used those arms in the past, then you may well be authorised to use them, providing you apply to the proper authorities with your proof. To prove such descent is not impossible, but very unlikely, and for the same reason that your family is probably not entitled to bear arms. What is that reason?

If your family had its own coat of arms, whether two or three generations back or twenty generations back, it is not something

Fig. 16.1 *A full achievement from an engraving of 1572, showing shield, helmet, wreath, crest, mantling, supporters, scroll and motto.*

your family is likely to have forgotten. You would already be aware of the fact. It would appear on old stationery, silverware and documents of some kind. Certainly your ancestors within living memory would know of it. The very fact that you have to ask the question at all, is almost certain evidence that no such coat of arms for your particular family exists.

A coat of arms was originally for recognition in the battlefield. It was painted on the shield of the owner, also on other items of his battle trappings. It is still usually depicted on a shield. The complete coat of arms, when drawn up correctly, consists of several items in addition to the shield itself, and is known in this full form as an 'achievement'. Immediately on top of the shield is positioned the helmet, which differs in metal and design according to rank. Above the helmet is a coloured cloth known as the 'mantling' and supposedly a relic of the days when a cloth cover kept the heat of the sun off the back of the helmet. The mantling is held in place by a wreath of the same twisted cloth. Above the wreath and on top of the helmet is the crest, and sometimes also a motto. Some achievements also incorporate supporters and a badge.

The use of supporters (such as a lion and unicorn) is almost entirely limited to certain members of the nobility.

A person (or a family) entitled to bear a coat of arms is said to be 'armigerous'. When a coat of arms is drawn up in its full splendour as, for instance, on a stained glass window, it will be in the form of its full achievement. When a coat of arms is mentioned in conversation, however, it is usually the shield itself which is intended, bearing as it does those features which make that particular coat individual. A shield might be drawn in various shapes, but for the convenience of displaying a coat of arms a broad form is most often used, such as in Fig. 16.2.

TERMINOLOGY AND CONVENTIONS

Most of the terms used in heraldry are based on Norman French, but the words are pronounced as if English (for instance *gules* is pronounced jools not zhule). The shield itself consists of a mixture of colours and metals, and the principal rule is that a colour must lie on a metal and vice versa; you may not place metal on metal or colour on colour. Colours and metals are visibly obvious in a painted achievement. However, for distinction in an uncoloured situation, such as an engraved coat of arms on a piece of silver plate, a method of shading was used to identify each colour and metal, and this is known as hatching. In British heraldry the colours and metals and their hatchings are as follows, but one must be careful to specify 'British' as some European countries hatched their colours differently.

In heraldry the term 'dexter' is used to mean right and 'sinister' left, but these terms apply as the shield might be described by a man holding it from behind, dexter being his right-hand position.

Argent *(ar. or arg.)*

Silver or white, in hatching
shown as a plain background.

Or

Gold or yellow, hatched as black
dots on a plain background.

Azure *(az.)*

Blue, hatched by
horizontal lines.

Gules *(gu.)*

Red, hatched by
vertical lines.

Purpure *(pu.)*

Purple, hatched by diagonal lines
from top right to bottom left
(facing the shield).

Sable *(sa.)*

Black, hatched by vertical and
horizontal lines together.

Vert *(ve.)*

Green, hatched by diagonal lines
from top left to bottom right
(facing the shield).

Fig. 16.2   *Indication of British heraldic colours by means of hatching.*

In an engraving therefore, where we see the shield from the front (the opposite side to the man holding it) dexter is on the left and sinister is on the right.

The devices on a shield are known as 'charges' and are of two main types – those consisting of a shape applied onto the shield (e.g., a bend or a chevron) and those consisting of smaller shaped objects (e.g., a fleur-de-lys or a lion). A coat of arms is described in heraldic language devised to convey an accurate representation of the shield and other parts of the achievement. Its precision is such that the exact devices on the shield are described closely, so are their precise positions on the shield, as well as their colours and metals.

There is quite a large heraldic language of terms and if you need to understand an heraldic description, you will almost certainly have to refer to a detailed reference book on the subject containing a glossary. Describing the arms in this correct way is known as 'blazoning'. The principle is that the background (the field) colour comes first, then the main charge, then lesser charges on the field, then lesser charges on the main charge. For instance: *gules, on a chevron or, three fleur-de-lys sable*, means a red shield on which is a gold chevron containing three black fleur-de-lys.

Fortunately the ability to sketch a coat of arms and perhaps to hatch in the colour coding may mean that you can manage, for your particular heraldic needs, without knowing the complicated language of blazoning.

The control of coats of arms today is in the hands of the Heralds, who have authority under the Queen both for the granting of new coats of arms and for recording details of those with rights to bear existing arms (the recording of the arms themselves and the genealogists of armigerous families). In England the College of Arms is situated in Queen Victoria Street, London. In Scotland the authority is the Lyon King of Arms, Lyon Office Records, New Register House, Edinburgh, EH1 3YT.

THE ARMIGEROUS FAMILY – HOW TO VERIFY IF IN DOUBT

If in your genealogical searches you find that your family runs into an armigerous one, in other words if your descent appears to be in the male line from an armigerous male, then you can apply to the College of Arms with your proof of descent for the right to bear those arms yourself, or perhaps a variation of them. Arms cannot pass down through a daughter, unless that daughter married a husband with his own arms, in which case the arms of the two families might be joined by quartering, that is, by dividing the shield in a specific way according to circumstances. Arms may have been quartered many times through numerous generations, which is why some arms can be such a complicated combination of numerous coats.

If your family has a coat of arms which has passed down through the male line for some generations, it is likely that you will already be well aware of the fact. Suppose, however, you come across an old letterheading amongst family papers of your grandfather or great grandfather and this proudly bears some sort of armorial device – an achievement, a shield displaying arms, or even a crest on its own. Is this really your coat of arms, and how do you check on this?

In Victorian times many a self-made gentleman had a fancy for a coat of arms. Some applied for a grant through the College of Arms, so what you find may have been one which was quite correctly granted to your ancestor in the late 19th century. Others however sketched up an impressive achievement and got the printer to include it on their letterheading. In other words they invented their own coats of arms, and of course people still sometimes do this today, much in the way that companies design a logo. The way to check on this is to approach the College of Arms to investigate the validity of any shield in question.

Perhaps you have amongst your cutlery some knives, forks or spoons bearing a crest; these were often engraved onto cutlery handles. Is the crest of *your* family, in other words, part of *your* coat of arms? Or is it the crest of some other family who once owned the cutlery? Or is it perhaps, just some invented, crest-like design put on the make the items look impressive when the neighbours came to dine? It might be possible for you to check on this in your local library by using one of several reference books there known as armorials. An armorial is simply a reference work containing coats of arms and their holders. Some are indexed by family name, some are indexed by the devices on the shield, some do both.

There are several classic works, many published in the nineteenth century, and these tend to be known by their popular names such as: Burke's *General Armory*, Papworth's *Armorial*, or Fairbairn's *Crests*. The full and correct titles will be found in the bibliography, Appendix D, page 184.

SEALS – BOUGHT OR INHERITED?

As you uncover certain legal documents concerning your family, you are likely to meet some which bear a seal, that is, an impression in sealing wax showing the imprint of a device. The word 'seal' signifies the hardened wax which carries the impression, the design or imprint left in the wax, and the metal object which made it – such as grandfather might have carried for decoration on his watch chain.

If you do come across such a document with your ancestor's signature and his 'seal' showing, say, a lion rampant, is it likely to be an impression of your ancestor's crest or badge, such as might be used in his coat of arms? No. Very unlikely.

It is true that in a document signed by the monarch or a nobleman, his seal may well have been his personal badge or crest.

The same could apply to a gentleman of an armigerous family. But for the majority of these seals, the device was impressed by any one of a box full of seals purchased by a solicitor or clerk and kept in the office to be used as needed for clients' documents.

It is quite possible that your ancestor had a personal seal of his own, which he bought because he liked the feeling of status it gave him. You might still have one somewhere in the family, and it could be interesting to attempt to identify it. But if the device is something as commonplace as a lion rampant you will find that there are so many as to make identification impossible. By and large such a seal is merely a form of imprint used to lend a more official and legally binding appearance to a document, and it will not help you in tracing your ancestry.

You will see that the question, posed earlier, of whether heraldry and genealogy are closely linked, has by now been answered. In other words, a knowledge of heraldry, fascinating though the subject is, is unlikely to help you in the task of tracing your ancestry except when you *know* your family is armigerous, or when you discover a long-lost coat of arms which proves to belong to one of your ancestors. In that happy event, you may well find that the College of Arms has a considerable pedigree concerning a branch of your family – and that is one area you will not then have to research yourself!

17   EMIGRANTS

An interest in genealogy is often stronger in those families whose ancestors left this country in the past (whether one generation ago or several) than in those who still live here. The countries mostly concerned are the English-speaking ones which at one time formed part of the British Empire: principally the United States of America, Canada, Australia, New Zealand and South Africa.

A resident in one of these countries today who wishes to trace his British ancestry and origins often has several advantages over someone who is a resident in Britain. First, the great majority of such emigrants from Britain went to their new countries in the nineteenth century, at a time when Civil Registration was already in operation in Britain. The countries themselves often set up their own Civil Registration system along the lines of the British system, but usually in much more detail. Emigrants were well aware that they were pioneers in what were 'new' countries, and they often felt a greater need to record their activities for posterity than those in the old country where such things were taken for granted.

Emigrants to these newer countries still had family ties with their country of origin, and regarded Britain as their 'old country'. They wrote home to their relatives, and often had strong memories of the area of Britain they had come from, of the kind of work their first emigrant ancestor did, and of conditions of life back in the old country. In short, nostalgia for Britain usually lingered for several generations, and of course still persists.

ESTABLISHING ORIGINAL LOCATION IN BRITAIN
For most such descendants of emigrant families who wish to trace their ancestry, there is no particular problem in going back over the period of time when they lived in the new country. Genealogical societies exist in virtually all of them and this is a factor which makes the task all the more straightforward. Those families who have written records of their place of origin in Britain can pick up the trail here just as easily as a British resident can today. For them the research procedures outlined in this book will apply according to the date of their ancestor's emigration. The problem for some will be in establishing exactly where in Britain the family lived prior to emigration, and it will be greater the further back in time the emigration took place. This kind of problem is likely to be greater for a present-day citizen of the United States of America than for a resident of one of the newer countries such as Canada. An American's ancestor may have emigrated several generations back when documentation was very uncertain, but a Canadian's ancestor probably emigrated only two or three generations back, when documentation was highly-detailed.

GENEALOGICAL SOCIETIES IN THE 'NEW' COUNTRY

The problem of establishing just where in Britain an emigrant ancestor originated is one that has beset researchers from the very beginning. Because of this the genealogical societies of the various countries have made a particular study of the problem. The genealogical society of a country will know of the existence and whereabouts of such records as passenger lists of emigrant ships, and may well have access to the published ones or indexes of emigrants. The first step for anyone hoping to trace the British origin of an emigrant ancestor therefore is to join the local genealogical or family history society for their own region or country. In Appendix D, page 185, some addresses are given for societies in the USA, Canada, Australia, New Zealand and South Africa.

In some of the countries of emigration census records exist of a considerably earlier date than for the British equivalents. Sometimes it may be known in advance at roughly what date the family left Britain, and this will apply especially in cases where the family is known to have established itself in the new country within the last three generations – for instance, if your father or grandfather was the emigrant. In such circumstances it is almost certainly known where the family lived in Britain before emigration. In other cases the family may have remained in contact with British cousins and this will make it easy for the location to be established.

Emigration at a time into the fourth generation or beyond will naturally involve the use of the census records of the country of residence, as well as the Civil Registration records, and any other sources, to help pinpoint the place of embarkation and of residence before emigration. Other facts will also need to be known, enough at least to enable the person to be identified as the right one when he has been located in British records. For example, a person's age at death in the new country would probably enable him to be identified provided his baptism could be located in Britain and his place of residence there already established. The chances of such identity are helped, of course, if the surname is an uncommon one.

If the ancestor's place of residence in Britain cannot be established, it may be impossible to trace the family origins further back – though if you are determined this will probably not stop you from trying. However if the surname is an unusual one, or even if the first name is very unusual and the surname not too commonplace, there are certain approaches to locating the British origin that can at least be attempted. The situation here facing the researcher is much the same as that where a trail has been lost in following back a British family – though with the British family one does at least know the later places of residence in Britain.

AN UNUSUAL SURNAME HELPS

Supposing an ancestor named Caleb Pogworthy is sought, who was known to have been living in Philadelphia in 1747. A search in the International Genealogical Index through the British counties, one by one, may well locate his origins, since there are unlikely to have been two such Caleb Pogworthys. Even if he was plain John Pogworthy there would still be a good possibility of recognising him once a likely baptismal entry was located. If the IGI proved unsuccessful, then with such an uncommon surname a search of probate indexes and an examination of all probates found in that surname might well reveal the will of a relative. Such a search for probates could be lengthy and the outcome uncertain and, with a more commonplace surname, probably pointless.

The possibility should not be overlooked that a person of British origin dying overseas and owning property in Britain may have had his will proved in British courts. With that in mind and, ideally some other clues too, a search of British probate records may be worth while. For instance, the ancestry was sought of one Robert King, a clockmaker of Washington, DC, America, known to have been working in the late 18th century. This is sketchy information indeed but a search of British probate courts was undertaken, using as a clue some of the known and recorded British clockmakers of the same surname on the offchance that one might be related. Eventually a will was found in the Prerogative Court of York of Robert King, clockmaker, of Scarborough, Yorkshire, proved in 1813. In the will he mentions various relatives including 'my son, Robert King, of Washington, America, clockmaker'. This was perhaps a lucky find and is unlikely to have been possible if trade continuity had not been guessed correctly.

The task of establishing whether the lists of ships' passengers, or of transported convicts, exist and their location can be daunting, but if you have decided to do it you will need to refer to one of the numerous special-subject books in the bibliography (Appendix D) according to the country and period involved.

Most people have at some time wondered about the origin of their surname – especially those who have unusual ones. If your name is Smith you probably don't spend too much time wondering about it. But if it's Ramsbottom, you probably do. Who was the first person to carry the name and how did he come to acquire it? Who was the first Mr Onions and why do you pronounce it 'on-eye-ons' and not 'onions' like the vegetable? Where did the first Mr. Sheepshanks come from? Why would anyone be named after the rear end of a ram or the legs of a sheep? Do such names have an entirely different origin from that which seems obvious?

In fact many names, which have a strange or amusing ring to them, may not have originated with the meaning they have today. To take Ramsbottom as an example, a 'bottom' was one old name for a valley floor, and the surname Ramsbottom may well have been used originally to describe a person who lived in the lower part of a valley, perhaps in a place known as Ramsbottom. Quite close to my home is a place named Ramsgill. A gill too was an old name for a valley. Someone named Ramsgill may quite possibly have taken the name from the place where he lived. Ramsgill would probably strike us as just another unusual surname; Ramsbottom would seem unusual and perhaps amusing simply because of the change of meaning of 'bottom'. When Shakespeare named one of his characters Bottom the word had already acquired its double meaning, perhaps even to the point where its original meaning was forgotten.

You may wonder whether you will be able to trace your surname back far enough to the very first ancestor to bear it, thus discovering its origin. The answer nearly always has to be 'no', and there are several reasons for this. It is true, of course, that there are a few exceptional cases where this *is* possible, but these are principally families whose surname is not of great age, that is, where the name itself began within the last four hundred years or so.

ORIGINS IT MAY BE POSSIBLE TO TRACE

An example of how that might happen would be in the case of an abandoned child, a foundling. Such a child would be taken into the care of the parish and, as its name was unknown, the parish overseers would themselves give it a name, sometimes based on the name of the parish itself and often with the nearest Saint's Day as a first name. Thus in 1705 young Samuel Lebow was apprenticed as a clockmaker to Richard George of London, Samuel being a child in the care of the parish of St. Mary le Bowe, London. This child was named by and after the parish of his finding, and if you traced your ancestry back to this man, you would have traced the root of your surname.

Another example, was the case of one Thomas Norweb, who was traced satisfactorily back to a point in the 1760s when he arrived in one village of many in which he resided in his particularly restless life. Prior to that time there appeared to be no such surname at all; the name did not exist in any of the innumerable records previously searched. Norweb happens to be an anagram of Browne and it seemed therefore that Thomas Norweb had deliberately changed his name from Browne to conceal his tracks from anyone seeking him – principally, of course, the law. After all, there were no laws on the choice of one's name, and this option was often taken by people seeking to move home to start a new life for whatever reason.

A further exception is the titled or wealthy land-owning family. Here a present-day researcher would have a better chance of going right back to origins because of evidence of bequests of goods and properties that his early ancestors might have made.

ORIGINS IT IS IMPOSSIBLE TO TRACE

Whatever the exceptions, most of us can expect that our surnames were fixed at a point far back in time, beyond the reach of the records we normally use to trace our ancestries – records which are largely dependent on the start of parish registers in 1538.

Not only do records not go back far enough to reach the origin of naming, but it is not reasonable to suppose that a surname had a single ultimate ancestor. If you are called Smith, you will not for one moment imagine that your ancestral line can be traced back to a single person named Smith, from whom all other Smiths descend. Clearly such a name would have numerous 'original ancestors', each one of whom might be the originator of a particular clan of Smith descendants. Even if your name is Ramsbottom, there may well have been more than one original named ancestor. So the idea of tracing your surname back to its point of origin is out of the question.

Yet there are books, even dictionaries, written about the origins of surnames in which you can look up almost any name and find out its 'origin'. In fact, what these books give you is the oldest documented example the compiler could find of the surname in question, where the example was located, and the likely meaning of the surname based on its oldest known spelling and location. What it is unlikely to tell you is that there are probably many other examples of that same surname as yet *un*documented, and that these may be spelt quite differently. With such knowledge (as yet unavailable of course) the suggested derivation of the name could be totally different. In any event, the supposed origin of the name, as offered from such a book, is no more than an educated guess.

Surnames for the bulk of the population began to be used during the 14th and 15th centuries, though at first these were not always fixed, but liable to change at each generation. Thus Adam, the son of John, might have been known widely as Adam Johnson. But his son, William, might have been known as William Adamson. This naming after the father is known as a patronymic surname. In Scotland the prefix Mac means 'son of'; in Norman French Fitz means the same, so that some names can readily be identified as patronymic.

The patronymic system of surnames was particularly strong in Celtic regions, notably Wales and Scotland. Welsh surnames especially were late in becoming fixed. Thomas's son Richard became Richard Thomas; Richard's son William became William Richards, and so on. In Wales the prefix ap indicated 'son of', which could produce such examples as William ap Rhys, developing into William Preece, William ap Robert into William Probert. Fixed surnames in Wales might not have occurred until the 16th century and even much later. Once surnames did become fixed in Wales there was a concentration of a few surnames (largely on account of their patronymic origins). A proliferation of names such as Jones, Evans and Davies only adds to other research difficulties there.

In Scotland there is a similar problem caused by patronymic origins (often with the preface Mac of course): it is the clan system. The clan system is very complicated and differs between Highland and Lowland Scots, for it is the Highlanders who were clansmen in the truest sense of the word. The clansmen were named after the chief, and while there might originally have been one Donald whose descendants took the name MacDonald (just as any English family would pass on the surname), here all others who sought allegiance or protection under the MacDonald banner also adopted the surname. This means that many who became MacDonald were totally unrelated to the MacDonald family and would have adopted the name at much later periods in history. Clans also had branches, known as septs, and the septs would often bear different surnames from the clan to which they bore allegiance. The overall position is ultimately similar to that in Wales, where the number of surnames is relatively few, thus making identification of particular individuals more difficult. Such difficulties are added to by such situations as the MacGregors, who earned such a bloodthirsty reputation that they were outlawed in 1603 and forbidden to use the name MacGregor until once more permitted to in 1775. For research procedures in Wales and Scotland see Chapter 12, page 122.

Other types of origin of surname are from the names of animals, plants, birds and natural objects: Bird, Fox, Tree, Crow, etc. Names of places form another category, though not always easy to recognise unless you are familiar with ancient placenames. They can be based on places which were the names of towns or villages – Dewsbury, Hastings, etc., – or ancient names meaning a clearing or a stream, such as Hurst or Lea or Brook. Occupations form another category – Shepherd, Farmer, Tiler, etc. Nicknames and familiar names form yet another – Redhead, Goodchild, Lightfoot. Often, therefore, it may be possible to identify the type of your surname, though many changes of spelling, pronunciation and meaning make this less easy than might first seem the case. However, it is not really relevant to the task of tracing your ancestry except that an uncommon name, or a name uncommon in a certain area, will always make the trail easier to follow.

The spelling of names

By the beginning of the sixteenth century, which coincides roughly with the beginning of parish registers, surnames were already fixed in England, though may not have been fixed for more than three or four generations before that. The parish registers were, for many families, the first occasions in which their names needed to be set down in writing, so the registers themselves would have fixed a certain form of spelling and they were there for constant reference. However, spelling was a variable factor and many names took generations for their spelling to become fixed. Now, in the registers, many a John Doe must have looked at the page and been pleased to see his name in written form. That was how it looked and how it was to be written.

For most of those tracing their ancestry the ability to recognise the name among a variety of haphazard spellings is the most important factor; that and the picking up of the trail as families moved from village to village. Certainly these are more urgent topics for the novice than theorising about how the name may have originated and whether it might be Anglo-Saxon or Norman-French.

The uses of 'alias'

Some features about surnames are important and may need to be understood during the genealogical research. One such is the use of an alias. Today the term suggests a criminal on the run, who changes his name to escape capture. In the past an alias meant simply an alternative name, sometimes, or perhaps at some former time, used by that person. An entry in a parish register may mention the alias as being one of the names by which that person was, or had formerly been, known. But it would be dangerous to make any assumption or inference as to why that person had used one; it could be for a quite legitimate reason.

Suppose Thomas Lightowler was born in 1675, the son of Richard and Janet. Suppose Richard died when Thomas was only four and his mother remarried. Her husband was Benjamin Shoesmith, who may have been a widower with a young family, surnamed Shoesmith of course. The family may have decided to name Thomas by the Shoesmith name, although he was Light-owler at birth. When Thomas married, or was buried, he might well have been written down as Thomas Shoesmith alias Light-owler. Thus an alias could hide a perfectly respectable name change. When Janet died she too might have been described as Janet Shoesmith alias Lightowler.

In the sixteenth century a widow who remarried might still be buried under the surname of her former, though long deceased, husband. For instance, if Janet Shoesmith had died in 1585 she might have been recorded as Janet Lightowler, especially if her second husband, Benjamin Shoesmith, had long been dead at the time of her death. How much more confusing if she had been recorded as Janet Lightowler, widow; it is true she once had been, but she had also been widowed again as Shoesmith. In such a situation the genealogist may be sufficiently confused to be thrown off the track altogether, and it is helpful to know in advance *some* of the possible reasons why people took on an alias. With a clearly-stated alias, such as the supposed burial of Janet Shoesmith alias Lightowler, all you can do as a researcher is to watch out thereafter for all entries in *both* surnames and hope that the reason for the alias may eventually become clear. At least be thankful that the alias was actually stated, giving you a clear indication of the two names to follow.

An alias may not crop up very often or occur in your family at all. You may think it would add a complication to the research, but in fact it should be regarded as a helpful clue. Far more complicated, and perhaps even unfathomable, would be a situation where a change of surname is undergone with no apparent reason. If our supposed Thomas Lightowler took his step-father's name of Shoesmith and married as Thomas Shoesmith, we would search in vain for the baptism of a Thomas Shoesmith, not having the clue to his baptised and born name which an alias would have provided.

It is just possible that a child born out of wedlock would be baptised in the mother's surname (as was usual) and yet the father's name may also be stated in the parish registers. So an alias giving two choices of surname might just refer to the surnames of both mother and father. This would be unusual but nevertheless possible.

In Scotland it was common practice to retain the maiden name of a man's wife even after her marriage. You might therefore find an apparent conflict of surnames in the entry for burial of Mary McLaren, wife of William Stewart, but what that means (in Scotland) is that William Stewart's wife, Mary (née McLaren), was buried. This practice was unusual in England except in very early periods (the 16th century for instance) but might always be a possibility in certain parishes, especially close to the Scottish border, where custom often overlapped.

An alias might have occurred in a case where the wish was to perpetuate the female surname, though more often this was achieved by uniting the two names as a double (hyphenated) name. If Reginald Witherspoon married Amelia Peck, who was the only surviving Peck child, the families may have wished to continue the Peck name by Reginald adopting the Peck name as an appendage to his own from the date of the marriage, thus becoming Reginald Witherspoon-Peck. The incentive to do this might be all the stronger if a substantial legacy of money or land would be coming Reginald's way. After the marriage Reginald, and his issue, might thereafter be known as Witherspoon-Peck, or even Witherspoon alias Peck, or possibly – depending on how insistent father-in-law Peck might be – Peck-Witherspoon or Peck alias Witherspoon. The hyphenated name is the more usual and researching a family tree will sooner or later unearth the point where the two names were united, which may well be at a time far beyond the recollection of present-day descendants.

UNUSUAL SURNAMES AND DISTRIBUTION

While you may find it fascinating to be able to identify which type of surname your own belongs to, it is not likely to assist you in the task of tracing your ancestry. But the desire to trace one's ancestry and the origins of a surname is often strongest in those whose surname is unusual.

Yet what may appear unusual as a surname in one area, probably that in which you live, may prove to be commonplace in a different one. An interesting exercise to find out just how unusual your surname is is to search the telephone directories of several areas of the country, which you can do in a large library. Even with a highly mobile population such as today's it can come as a surprise to realise how settled a large section of the population has been, even during the last hundred years, and before that, the population was much more static anyway. My own surname, for example, is very unusual in Yorkshire, where I was born and still live, but the telephone directories of Leicestershire and Lincoln-shire where my name originated show a much higher concentra-tion. So to some degree telephone directories do reflect original surname distribution even four hundred years after families began to drift elsewhere. An exception perhaps is London, which always acted as a magnet to everyone, so gives a more distorted picture.

Telephone directories are no more (for our purpose) than a massive index of names showing current distribution. Such indexes are often of vital aid to the genealogist, particularly in helping him pick up a lost trail when the place of origin of a migrating ancestor is unknown. The International Genealogical Index is one such index ideally suited to origin-finding.

SURNAME VARIATIONS

Confusion can often be caused by seeing a name similar to one's own but spelt differently. If your surname were Taylor, you would today be unlikely to regard anyone whose name was spelt as Tailor, Taylour, Tayler or even Talor as being of the same family or even group of families. However, two points have to be borne in mind. First, the records you may consult were rarely, if ever, written by your ancestor, but by some other person, who was doing his best to spell the name as he heard it pronounced. (He may have been deaf, illiterate, or have written with a trembling hand – or all three.) When the next person copied out this name he may have mis-spelt what he too misread.

Today you might spell out your surname to a clerical official who writes it down and gets it wrong, but there's a good chance you can correct it. In the past many people could not read or write, and could do no more than speak their surname aloud and rely on the clerk to write it down as he saw fit. Add to this the problem of mispronunciation and strong local dialects and you will realise why there is so much variation between spellings of the same name.

You are also likely to come across documents where your ancestor signed with his mark because he could not write. As you go back in time this likelihood increases. Some estimates suggest that in the mid-18th century less than half the population could write their own names. Therefore you must constantly be on the lookout for mis-spelt versions of your name, and for mis-spelt placenames too.

Some people drop their h's. A man called Heaton might pronounce it Eaton. It could easily appear in written form as Heeton, Heyton, Heighton, Heton, Eaton, Eatern, or all manner of permutations. Not only might you fail to recognise your name when faced with a mis-spelt version of it, but if you were searching an index under H for Heaton, you would miss it completely if it were correctly indexed under E from its written form of Eaton. So at all times you must be on the lookout for possible mis-indexed forms, especially if you have failed to find the desired information in its correctly-spelt form in the place where it should be. Spelling variations are likely to be less of a problem in the 19th century but become progressively worse as you work back in time.

Not only were h's sometimes dropped, they were sometimes inserted where they shouldn't have been. In tracing the family of Ismay I was surprised to find it written on one occasion as Hismay and even signed (it was a will) by the man himself as Hismay. Obviously he was putting on his Sunday best accent for the benefit of the lawyer. On another occasion I was tracing a family named Ogden when I came across a few parish register entries written (by the clerk) as Hogden, and then n is-read and mis-indexed under Hagden. It takes a lively imagination to check an index for Hagden when looking for Ogden.

19 SEARCH SEQUENCE CHECKUP AND RECOVERING A LOST TRAIL

As we said in the beginning, the point at which you start your research depends upon how much information is available from family documents. This varies from family to family, but generally you would begin with confirming your oldest data around mid- to late-19th century. Searches carried out in the order described ensure that you avoid spending time on any type of record before you know exactly what you want from it.

Let us recap on the recommended order, but note that *this list is not identical with the one on pages 13–14* because certain steps, like joining your local history society, and acquiring maps, are one-off processes that won't be repeated. Also the order of 5 and 6 can be interchangeable, depending on the results you have achieved, and the point at which you have arrived in your researches.

1. Family papers The first step, as described in Chapter 1, is to gather such factual or legendary, information as you can from family members, record important data and obtain sight of documents such as family bibles and certificates of birth, marriage and death. Sketch your information into a first rough pedigree. Even though the pedigree may change considerably at each stage, this early one is important as a cross-check as is each of the provisional ones you make.

2. Civil Registration From the General Register Office, or the local Register Office, search and obtain certificates of birth and marriage (perhaps death too), as described in Chapter 2. These will provide you with positive anchor points post-1837, and take you, ideally, close to the census dates of 1851 or 1861. If they fail to pinpoint your family accurately enough for these census searches, use directories of around these dates, especially if you need to locate a precise address in a city.

3. Census Returns If you can locate your family in that of 1851 and/or 1861, that will take you back furthest, as described in Chapter 3. The 1841 census is less precise in its information, but don't neglect it as it may help you pick up an ancestor who died before 1851. The censuses of 1871 and later may also help and you should note all members of your family you can locate. Errors of listing in one census are often corrected in the next, ten years later. With such a sequence of censuses available you will probably pick up two generations, each with children, and possibly side-lines of the second generation too.

4. Parish Registers and the IGI These are normally your next point of call after censuses, as described in Chapter 4. From them you will, unless very unlucky or dealing with a highly mobile family, make considerable progress. In this category are included nonconformist registers where applicable.

5. Wills and Probate Records By this stage you should have enough data about parts of your family tree to make a thorough searching of probate records worth while. This includes all probates in the required surname, unless it is exceptionally popular in that area. Chapters 10 and 11 deal with these processes in detail.

6. Marriage Licences and Other Records From this point on it is a matter of assessing what has so far emerged and planning further researches accordingly. This is the time to put a little more flesh onto the bare bones of your pedigree by using other kinds of records such as Court Rolls, Quarter Sessions records and the like. Or it may be more appropriate to revert to parish registers of other parishes. At this point your experience will enable you to assess for yourself the direction of further inquiries.

You may need to return to some of the categories of record used earlier for further searches in the light of your total findings. Also you may reach a block where your searches fail to produce the desired leads. Your approach to solving the problem of a lost trail will depend on the circumstances and the period, but the following courses of action may be helpful.

RECOVERING A LOST TRAIL

Sooner or later the laws of diminishing returns may apply as the results from continuing searches produce less and less, or even nothing at all. When this happens it may be that you have gone as far as you can hope.

On the other hand, there may be ways round the problem. If even one new fact has come to light since your earlier stages of search, perhaps you should consider re-searching some of those records again in the light of this? Back-tracking at any point may assist you in going forward. The following is a list of suggestions, any of which might help you recover a lost trail. They are not in any special order.

Review Before you strike out wildly at optimistic searches of a general nature, review your position. How stuck are you? What sort of information would assist? Spend a little time scanning back through your progress to date. Have you made any errors or jumped to conclusions that might be false? If you had known at the time of earlier searching (censuses, registrations, parish registers, wills, etc.) what you know now, might you have looked out for other items? Is it perhaps worth going back to these records to do this?

International Genealogical Index This can be a marvellous tool for helping to locate an unknown parish of origin as it enables wide expanses of territory to be covered at once. You can thus pinpoint those parishes where families of the same surname concentrated, including perhaps the one where your own originated. But bear in mind the IGI's deficiencies, its possible errors and its potentially incomplete coverage, even of a parish which is included. Remember it can be used to search adjacent counties as well as adjacent parishes, but remember too that it is weakest on marriages and burials.

Registers of neighbouring parishes   One recognised procedural step is to search neighbouring parishes one by one in an ever-widening circle around that in which the family trail ran out. If the surname fails to appear at all in these, this may be a clue that the family moved here from some much greater distance, and there comes a point where this type of search has to be dropped in favour of another approach.

Nonconformity   Neighbouring parish registers to be searched should also include nearby nonconformist registers, even if there has so far been no sign of nonconformity in your family. They may only have been nonconformists *for a certain period* of their lives, or they may have stood as sponsors or witnesses for nonconformist friends or relations.

Late baptism   Always extend the period for a missing baptism well into that person's adult life. Some were baptised as adults, perhaps shortly before marriage, for example. Sometimes a family whose church attendance had lapsed might present a whole group of children for baptism on the same day, even with the older children well into their teens. This might happen particularly with a family newly moved into a parish. With large families they may well have forgotten who had been baptised and who had not, and might decide to baptise all of them just to be sure – in which case some children would have been baptised twice!

Probate lists   You should have a list of all probates in the required surname, as a search of the wills of such people may throw up one who proves to be related. If nothing else they will indicate the spread of the surname in the area of interest or origin.

Published registers   Published parish registers exist for certain parishes in most counties. These are usually indexed and are easy to search quickly, therefore may help in scanning for a surname in the area. Marriage indexes can also be most helpful.

Other local records   In each county there is usually a record office or local archaeological society with *specialist* indexed data. See what they have and scan through such indexes as are available. If such items are on open shelves it may be that an hour spent scanning some of them will offer clues. Some have will abstracts or newspaper items/abstracts, deeds, court rolls, poll books, hearth tax returns, oath rolls (such as allegiance to Crown or Church), rates books, or even directories.

Telephone directories Modern telephone directories can, surprisingly, offer a guide to the region of origin for an uncommon name. If you have lost the county of origin these are certainly worth a try, as even in modern times the highest concentration of an unusual name still tends to be in its main county of origin. London however has attracted people from everywhere, so London directories are not nearly so helpful.

County histories It may be worth while looking through some of those which exist for each county or region. The families mentioned in them may only be the more wealthy and influential ones, but there is always a chance that yours is an offshoot of one. In any event the local trades and industries of the area, and the indications of population movements within them, may well provide leads.

Side-lines and female lines A good idea can be to look more closely at female lines (uncles, aunts, cousins of a bride), even though you may not regard them as of prime importance in your search. Wills of such people may given clues to the origins of the groom's ancestry. The same applies to offshoots of the male line – uncles and the female connections of an uncle's bride for instance.

Witnesses Those who stood as witnesses, sponsors, overseers of wills and trustees, were not picked out of the blue. They were often relatives and it might be worth pursuing their genealogy for a while to see whether leads emerge into your own main family. Even if they prove to be unrelated, their movements and places of origin may well coincide with your ancestor's.

Maps An hour or two pondering over maps of the period may help at such a time of difficulty. Bridges and roads can be followed. Market towns may have been magnets. Canals and rivers may have been used as travel links rather than roads.

Trade connections Unless they were general labourers our ancestors did not change trades with any frequency. If your ancestor was a quarryman, search for the nearest quarries he may have worked before the present one. Gamekeepers, shepherds, woodmen, blacksmiths . . . try thinking as they must have thought when moving employ. A blacksmith, for instance, would try to locate himself in a market town, or beside a main highway, to take advantage of passing trade. Often common sense will lead you in the right direction. Seldom would farm workers have originated in towns, though by the start of the 19th century rural workers were increasingly drawn into towns as factories offered new prospects. Trades very often passed from father to son through several generations.

20 THE PROFESSIONALS AND WHERE TO FIND THEM

At various points in the book I have mentioned that you may want to call upon professional help at some time, especially, for instance, when you are in the preliminary stages of your Civil Registration searches and you live a long way from the General Register Office in London (Chapter 2). I have also said that when you reach the 18th century you may find that the county where your family lived is too distant for you easily to visit the record office in person. In both instances it would be more efficient and less costly for you to employ an agent.

What kind of professional agent should you look for? Where is he or she to be found?

THE PROFESSIONALS AND HOW THEY WORK

There is a difference between a genealogist and a record agent (or record searcher).

A *genealogist* is one who will plan the whole research programme and decide, on the basis of the original facts set before him, exactly how to set about tracing your ancestry. He will plot out each step in turn and direct all operations, using his experience and judgement as to how best he should spend your money. He may conduct all searches himself or, more likely, he will employ a record searcher for those documents located inconveniently distant from his base.

A *record searcher*, or *agent*, is a person who usually conducts searches at a particular record office or archives repository at the request of the person planning the research. A record searcher may be instructed to search a specific record for specific facts, or be allowed to vary the action according to what emerges. All such searches are arranged on a financial basis mutually agreeable to the searcher and planner, often with a stipulation not to spend more than a certain amount of time on a particular search – an hour or two, or a day or two, according to what is involved. In the interests of economy for all concerned the fullest use should be made of any one visit to a record office, so a searcher may be able to conduct work for two or three different clients on the same visit. Everything depends on cases in hand at the time.

In practice a genealogist may also act in the capacity of a record searcher if he is asked, and if his work load permits. In practice too a record searcher who has perhaps worked on the records of a certain region for many years, and will be very familiar with local genealogical work, may suggest the course of action most likely to trace the next link in the pedigree.

By and large you are hoping to act for yourself as overall planner of the campaign, and you will probably want to ask for a specific search to be made in a particular set of records. Any researcher will usually be willing to do this for you, for his rate of fees, whether he styles himself genealogist, record searcher or record agent. If he or she already has too much work in hand, you will have to approach your second choice.

Some genealogists, perhaps the better ones who are kept busiest, will not take on your problems at the point where you get stuck. It often happens that someone tracing his own ancestry will reach a point where he can get no further, struggle for a while, then admit defeat and pack up a bundle of document copies and post it to a genealogist explaining that he has done all the spade-work and would just like the professional to finish it off for him. Not many professionals like that kind of case and some will refuse it outright, as I have myself in the past – unless it was an especially interesting case. There are several reasons for this.

If it is simply that the amateur has run out of knowledge and doesn't know where to turn for further leads, a professional may be happy to take over and carry on from his greater experience. But the big worry is that the amateur may have made some error in his pedigree so far, causing him to be thrown off the scent; he may have been careless in searching one particular record and so has missed a vital clue; or he may have searched indexed records instead of a full search and missed something vital which was mis-indexed or omitted from the index altogether. This can be a headache.

However, a genealogist who takes on a case from the very beginning knows exactly what records he has searched and how thoroughly. One who takes on a case partway through cannot have that certainty and may have to insist on re-searching some of the records himself.

Some professionals are expert in certain older scripts, which the amateur just cannot learn to read. You can always turn for this sort of translation help when you need to, on a job-by-job basis if you wish. Most professionals enjoy their work and are more than willing to be helpful and accommodating to anyone who approaches them. So when the point comes that you need professional help, how do you find it?

FINDING THE RIGHT PROFESSIONALS – FURTHER SOCIETIES OF INTEREST

In almost every record office a regular group of researchers may be seen attending frequently. Some are full-time professionals, some are retired people doing part-time paid research work as a pleasurable pastime. The staff of most repositories are not available themselves to carry out research work, though they may obligingly look up a single item if requested by post. For the convenience of enquirers and to relieve themselves of a lot of queries they cannot deal with, most record offices have drawn up a list of local people who are willing to search records for a fee. If you write to the record office, and enclose return postage, they will send you a copy of their list of names. They will not 'recommend' a particular person but will leave the choice to you. You will also have to arrange the fee with the agent yourself.

In the 1960s an association of professionals was formed, the Association of Genealogists and Record Agents, known as AGRA. Only experienced researchers are allowed to join and the association attempts to maintain high standards of conduct and expertise among its members. The membership is scattered throughout Britain and you should easily be able to find a member close to the area where you require research.

If you would like a copy of the Society's list of members, you should write to them (enclosing a stamped addressed envelope, as always) at:

> The Association of Genealogists and Record Agents
> 1 Woodside Close
> Caterham
> Surrey CR3 6AU

For Scotland you should write to:

> The Scottish Association of Genealogists and Record
>   Agents
> 106 Brucefield Avenue
> Dunfermline
> KY11 4S7

If you need help in tracing your Scottish ancestsors you should approach:

> The Scots Ancestry Research Society
> 20 York Place
> Edinburgh EH1 3EP

In the Introduction (page 9), I gave details about the Society of Genealogists and the many resources and services it offers all genealogists from novices to experts. Don't forget its quarterly publication, the 'Genealogists' Magazine', which runs advertisements from professional researchers all over the country. This could be of great help to you.

An organisation which undertakes genealogical research, and offers many more facilities too is the Institute of Heraldic and Genealogical Studies, founded in 1961. It is an educational and charitable trust whose object is the history and structure of the family, and it runs correspondence courses in genealogy and related subjects. It has its own specialised library, publishes a series of parish register maps, and offers for sale all publications on genealogy. A list of these, plus other information, will be sent on application.

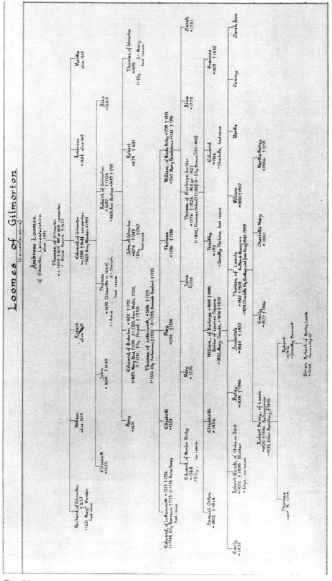

Fig. 20   *A complete pedigree, drawn up by a professional calligraphist.*

Loomes of Gilmorton (Leicestershire)

Armorial Bearings used by John Loomes of Braintree

Blazon: Argent, between two pallets gules, three fleurs-de-lys in pale, a chief azure. Crest: On a chapeau a pelican vulning herself proper.

John Loomes of Braintree, Essex, † 1619

Ambrose Loomes of Gilmorton, Leicestershire, alive 1591

Thomas of Gilmorton b.1565 †1618 carpenter m. Alice Harris † 1623

Sources:
Family papers
Parish Registers of Gilmorton, Lutterworth, Kimcote, Robertson, South Kilworth, Hinckley, Fenny Drayton, and Higham-on-the-Hill, in Leicestershire, and of Monks Kirby, in Warwickshire.
Wills & Memorial Rolls of Leicester Record Office.
Settlement Certs & Hearth Taxes, at Warwick Record Office.
Marriage Licences, at Leicester Museum.
Census Returns, 1841/51/61.

Abbreviations:
b. born, m. married, † died pr. proved, will without

Compiled by:
B. Loomes, B.A. Genealogist
24 Cragg Brook View, Cragg Rise, Morley, Leeds, Yorks.

Drawn by:
A. Robinson, I.eng, F.R.S.A., Heraldist & Genealogist (Corporate)

The Institute of Heraldic and Genealogical Studies
Northgate
Canterbury
Kent CT1 1BA

A recently-founded, non-profit-making society formed to assist anyone tracing British or Irish ancestors is the Family History Club of Great Britain. It publishes a bi-monthly magazine, 'Family Twigletts' and an annual directory, *Family History Knowledge UK*, the purpose of which is to enable members to make contact and exchange information with others working on similar projects, as well as to provide a mass of potentially useful information to the researcher. Write for information to:

The Family History Club of Great Britain
19 Penybryn
Mountain Ash
Glamorgan CF45 3TJ

From these varying sources you should have no difficulty in finding a researcher to assist you. And when your task is ended, you may wish to have your pedigree drawn up by a professional calligraphist. You will get the names of a number of these from AGRA or the 'Genealogists' Magazine'.

Computer Software for Genealogy

Today many people own personal computers and use them for word processing as well as for specific programming. In genealogical research the word processor is invaluable for generating letters, making record entries, storing material, filing information, keeping lists, and many other things. On the program side, software systems designed for different aspects of family research are available commercially. If you decide to invest in one, your choice will largely be governed by the type and extent of research you intend to do.

You do not actually *need* a computer to carry out excellent and productive genealogical research; you can manage perfectly well with pencil and paper. But in a world where computers play increasingly important roles in people's homes and workplaces, and are capable of ever more sophisticated operations in organising and analysing information, it makes sense for the genealogist to look at the advantages they offer. Indeed it is often said that the use of a computer can make a genealogist more systematic and critical.

If you already own a computer, your choice of software will largely be governed by what is compatible with it. If you do not own a computer, but are thinking of buying one, you will need guidance on obtaining the best equipment for running the software of your choice.

All major genealogical organisations put out excellent information on computer software packages, and a large number of books and journals are available from many sources.

For the genealogist with no previous knowledge of computers, perhaps the best of the small introductory books is *Computers for Family History* published by

Hawgood Computing Ltd, 26 Cloister Road, London W3 0DE.

The text is written in simple, straightforward style, and divided into three main sections: the first deals with computer models suitable for genealogy, and some of the software that can be run on them; the second discusses the types of information genealogists need to store, and ways in which computers can store it; the third outlines some of the programs and software available – database packages, word processing packages and genealogy packages. The book also contains lists of books and magazines for further reading, details of relevant clubs and societies, and other useful addresses.

The Society of Genealogists publish a quarterly magazine 'Computers in Genealogy' (started in 1982) which contains a wealth of practical information and is available from the Society of Genealogists (address on page 9). The Society also issues a leaflet

'Assessing Computer Software for Genealogical Use'.

Arguments against the use of computers are generally along the lines that they can introduce mistakes such as mis-spelt names. Of course this may happen, but it is not the computer which is at fault; it is the operator. Even the most sophisticated software package is only as good as its operator and it cannot correct mistakes fed into it.

In genealogy there is a further pitfall. We have seen how variants in the spellings of names through the centuries can be very extreme. Fiennes, for example, could originally have been written in numerous ways – Fins, Fens, Fans, Vins, Vens, etc. Unless all your references are stored with all their possible variants, including some which you cannot predict in advance, no single reference to the computer's index will bring up those variants – and you may miss a vital clue. The machine can only recognise what you ask it to recognise, and not the unexpected versions that you would quickly spot in your handwritten notes on a particular search.

In order to cater for everyone, the present book is written on the assumption that your family research processes will be carried on, and recorded, without the use of a computer. This method has served genealogists well for many generations, and will doubtless do so for generations to come. It is entirely up to you to decide how far you want to bring technology into your researches – or if you want to bring it into them at all.

SOME USEFUL SOCIETIES

Anglo-Jewish Association (and Museum), Woburn House, Upper Woburn Place, London WC1H 0EP

Association of Genealogists and Record Agents, 1 Woodside Close, Caterham, Surrey CR3 6AV

Catholic Family History Society (Mrs B. Murray), 2 Winscombe Crescent, London W5 1AZ

College of Arms, Queen Victoria Street, London WC2R 1LP

Family History Club of Great Britain, 19 Penybryn, Mountain Ash, Mid-Glamorgan CF45 3TJ

Federation of Family History Societies, Benson Room, Birmingham and Midland Institute, Margaret Street, Birmingham B3 3BS

Guild of One-Name Studies, PO Box G, 14 Charterhouse Buildings, Goswell Road, London EC1M 7BA

Huguenot Society, 54 Knatchbull Road, London SE5 9QY

Institute of Heraldic and Genealogical Studies, Northgate, Canterbury, Kent CT1 1BA

Scottish Association of Genealogists and Record Agents, 106 Brucefield Avenue, Dunfermline, KY11 4S7

Scots Ancestry Research Society, 20 York Place, Edinburgh EH1 3EP

Scottish Genealogical Society, 9 Union Street, Edinburgh EH1 3LT

Society of Friends, Friends' House, Euston Road, London NW1 2BJ

Society of Genealogists, 14 Charterhouse Buildings, Goswell Road, London EC1M 7BA

See also page 185.

RECORD OFFICES

This lists the major County Record Offices (CROs) in England, Wales and Scotland, based on the old county boundaries.

ENGLAND

Bedfordshire Bedfordshire Record Office, County Hall, Bedford MK42 9AP

Berkshire Berkshire Record Office, Shire Hall, Reading RG2 9XD

Buckinghamshire Buckinghamshire Record Office, County Hall, Aylesbury HP20 1UA

Cambridgeshire Cambridgeshire County Record Office, Shire Hall, Cambridge CB3 0AP

Cheshire Cheshire Record Office, Duke Street, Chester CH1 1RL

    Wirral Archives Service, Central Library, Borough Road, Birkenhead L41 2XB

    Stockport Archive Service, Central Library, Wellington Road South, Stockport SK1 3RS

    Tameside Archive Service, Stalybridge Library, Trinity Street, Stalybridge SK16 2BN

Cornwall Cornwall Record Office, County Hall, Truro TR1 3AY

Cumberland Cumbria Record Office, The Castle, Carlisle CA3 8UR

Derbyshire Derbyshire Record Office, County Offices, Matlock DE4 3AG

Devon Devon Record Office, Castle Street, Exeter EX4 3PU

    West Devon Record Office, Unit 3 Clare Place, Coxside, Plymouth PL4 0JW

    North Devon Record Office, North Devon Library, Tuly Street, Barnstaple EX32 7EJ

Dorset Dorset Record Office, County Hall, Dorchester DT1 1XJ

Durham Durham Record Office, County Hall, Durham DH1 5UL

    Durham University Library, Archives and Special Collections, 5 The College, Durham DH1 3EQ

Essex Essex Record Office, County Hall, Chelmsford CM1 1LX

    Essex Record Office (Colchester Branch), Stanwell House, Stanwell Street, Colchester, Essex CO2 7DL

    Essex Record Office (Southend Branch), Central Library, Victoria Avenue, Southend on Sea SS2 6EX

Gloucestershire Gloucestershire Record Office, Clarence Row, Gloucester GL1 3DW

    Bristol Record Office, Council House, Bristol BS1 5TR

Hampshire Hampshire Record Office, 20 Southgate Street, Winchester SO23 9EF

    Southampton City Records Office, Civic Centre, Southampton SO9 4XR

    Portsmouth City Records Office, 3 Museum Road, Portsmouth PO1 2LE

Crawley Family History Centre
Old Horsham Road
Crawley, Sussex RH11 8PD
Telephone: 0293 516151

Douglas Family History Centre
Woodside Woodburn Road
Isle of Man, UK
Telephone: 0624 75834

Dublin Family History Centre
Ireland Dublin Mission
The Willows, Finglass, Dublin 11
Telephone: 010 353 4625609

Dundee Family History Centre
Bingham Terrace
Dundee, Tayside
Telephone: 0382 451247

Edinburgh Family History Centre
30A, Colinton Road
Edinburgh 10
Telephone: 031 337 3049

Forest of Dean
Wynols Hill, Queensway
Coleford, Gloucestershire

Glasgow Family History Centre
35 Julian Avenue, Glasgow
Strathclyde G12
Telephone: 041 357 1024

Helston Family History Centre
Clodgey Lane, Helston
Cornwall

Huddersfield Family History Centre
2 Halifax Street, Birchencliffe
Huddersfield, West Yorkshire
HD3 8BY
Telephone: 0484 420352

Hyde Park Family History Centre
64/68 Exhibition Road
South Kensington
London SW7 2PA
Telephone: 071 589 8561

Hull Family History Centre
Hull 2nd Ward
725 Holderness Road
Hull, Yorks (temporary)
Telephone: 0482 794250

Ipswich Family History Centre
42 Sidegate Lane West
Ipswich, Suffolk 1PA 3DB
Telephone: 0473 723 182

Kirkaldy Family History Centre
Winifred Crescent/Forth Park
Kirkcaldy, Fife
Telephone: 0592 640041

Leeds Family History Centre
Vesper Road
Leeds, West Yorkshire LS5 3QT
Telephone: 0532 585297

Leicester Family History Centre
Thorpe Hill, Alan Moss Road
Loughborough, Leicester
Telephone: 0509 214991

Lichfield Family History Centre
Purcell Avenue, Lichfield, Staffs.
Telephone: 0543 262 621

Liverpool Family History Centre
4 Mill Bank, Liverpool
Merseyside L13 0BW
Telephone: 051 228 0433

Maidstone Family History Centre
76B London Road
Maidstone, Kent ME16 0DR
Telephone: 0622 757811

Manchester Family History Centre
Altrincham Road, Wythenshawe
Manchester M22 4BJ
Telephone: 061 902 9279

Mansfield Family History Centre
Southridge Drive, Mansfield
Nottinghamshire NG18 4FT
Telephone: 0623 26729

Merthyr Tydfil
Family History Centre
Nanty Gwenith Street
George Town
Merthyr Tydfil
Telephone: 0685 722455

Munster Family History Centre
The Willows, Fingerlass
Dublin 11, Ireland
Telephone: 0001 212625 Mission
Home; 0001 306899 Office; or 0001
306637

Newcastle-Under-Lyme
Family History Centre
The Brampton
Newcastle-Under-Lyme
Staffs. ST5 0TV
Telephone: 0782 620653

Newport Isle of Wight
Family History Centre
Chestnut Close, Shide Road
Newport, Isle of Wight
Telephone: 0983 529643

Northampton
Family History Centre
137 Harlestone Road
Northampton NN5 6AA
Telephone: 0604 587630

Norwich Family History Centre
19 Greenways, Eaton
Norwich, Norfolk
Telephone: 0603 52440

Nottingham Family History Centre
Hempshill Lane, Bulwell
Nottingham NG6 8PA
Telephone: 0602 274194

Paisley Scotland
Family History Centre
Campbell Street, Johnstone
Strathclyde PA5 8LD
Telephone: 0505 20886

Peterborough
Family History Centre
Cottesmore Close off Atherstone
Netherton Estate,
Peterborough

Plymouth Family History Centre
Hannamead Road
Plymouth, Devon
Telephone: 0752 668666

Poole Family History Centre
8 Mount Road, Parkstone
Poole, Dorset
Telephone: 0202 730 646

Portsmouth Family History Centre
Kingston Crescent
Portsmouth, Hampshire
Telephone: 0705 696 243

Rawtenstall Family History Centre
Haslingden Road, Rawtenstall
Rossendale, Lancs.
Telephone: 0706 213 460

Reading Family History Centre
280 The Meadway, Tilehurst
Reading, Berkshire
Telephone: 0731 410211

Redditch Family History Centre
321 Evesham Road, Crabbs Cross
Redditch, Worcestershire B97 5JA
Telephone: 0527 550657

Romford Family History Centre
64 Butts Green Road, Hornchurch
Essex RM11 2JJ
Telephone: 04024 58412

St. Albans Family History Centre
London Road at Cutenhoe Road
Luton, Bedfordshire
Telephone: 0582 22242

St. Helier Family History Centre
Rue de la Vallee, St. Mary
Jersey, C.I.
Telephone: 0534 82171

Sheffield Family History Centre
Wheel Lane, Grenoside
Sheffield, Yorkshire S30 3RL
Telephone: 0742 453231

Staines Family History Centre
41 Kingston Road
Staines, Middlesex TW14 0ND
Telephone: 0784 453823

Sunderland Family History Centre
Linden Road
off Queen Alexandra Road
Sunderland, Tyne & Wear
England
Telephone: 091 5285787

Sutton Coldfield
Family History Centre
185 Penns Lane
Sutton Coldfield, Birmingham
Telephone: 021 384 2028

Swansea Family History Centre
Cockett Road, Swansea
W. Glamorgan

Wandsworth Family History Centre
149 Nightingale Lane
Balham, London SW12
Telephone: 081 673 6741

Worthing Family History Centre
Goring Street
Worthing, West Sussex

Yate Family History Centre
Wellington Road
Yate, Avon
Telephone: 0454 323004

York Family History Centre
West Bank, Acomb
York, Yorkshire
Telephone: 0904 785 128

BIBLIOGRAPHY

GENERAL GUIDES

Camp, A. J., *Tracing your Ancestors* (John Gifford 1970).

Clare, W., *Simple Guide to Irish Genealogy* (Irish Genealogical Research Society 1967).

Colwell, S., *The Family History Book* (Phaidon 1983).

Field, D. M., *Tracing Your Ancestors* (Treasure Press 1991).

Hamilton-Edwards, G., *In Search of Ancestry* (Phillimore 1983).

Hawgood, D., *Computers for Family History – an Introduction* (Hawgood Computing Ltd, London 1989).

Matthews, C. M., *Your Family History* (Lutterworth Press 1991).

Pelling, G., *Beginning your Family History* (Federation of Family History Societies 1990).

Smith, F. and Gardner, D. E., *Genealogical Research in England and Wales*, three volumes (Bookcraft, Utah 1964).

Steel, D., *Discovering your Family History* (BBC Books 1989).

Tate, W., *The Parish Chest* (Cambridge University Press 1985).

Whyte, D., *Introducing Scottish Genealogical Research* (Scottish Genealogical Society 1982).

Willis, A. J. and Tatchell, M., *Genealogy for Beginners* (Phillimore 1984).

GENERAL DIRECTORIES

Caley, I. L., *National Genealogical Directory* (annually).

Park, K. and T., *Family History Knowledge UK 1991* (Family History Club of Great Britain, annually).

Johnson, K. A. and Sainty, M. R., *Genealogical Research Directory* (published in Australia annually).

CENSUS

Gibson, J. S. W., *Census Returns 1841–1881 on Microfilm* (Federation of Family History Societies 1990).

Gibson, J. S. W., *Marriage, Census and other Indexes for Family Historians* (Federation of Family History Societies 1988).

MAPS

Adams, C., *Guide to the Antique Shops of Britain* (Antique Collectors' Club annually).

Humphery-Smith, C., *The Phillimore Atlas and Index of Parish Registers* (Phillimore 1984).

Lister, R., *How to Identify Old Maps and Globes* (Bell 1965).

Tooley, R. V., *Maps and Map-makers* (Bonanza Books, New York 1962).

RECORD OFFICES

Gibson, J. S. W. and Peskett, P., *Record Offices – how to find them*

(Federation of Family History Societies 1991).

Royal Commission on Historical Manuscripts, *Record Repositories in Great Britain* (HMSO 1982).

PARISH REGISTERS

Fullarton, A., *The Parliamentary Gazetteer of England and Wales* (Fullarton & Co 1850 and later editions)

Gibson, J. S. W., *Bishops' Transcripts and Marriage Licences* (Federation of Family History Societies 1991).

Gibson, J. S. W., *Marriage, Census and other Indexes for Family Historians* (Federation of Family History Societies 1988).

Gibson, J. S. W. and Walcot, M., *Where to find the International Genealogical Index* (Federation of Family History Societies 1985).

Rogers, C. D., *The Family Tree Detective* (Manchester University Press 1989).

Steel, D. J. (and others), *National Index of Parish Register Copies* (Society of Genealogists 1966 continuing). Several volumes are already published. Eventually volumes to cover the whole country will be issued.

NONCONFORMISTS

Breed, G. R., *My Ancestors were Baptists: how can I find out more about them?* (Society of Genealogists 1988).

Gandy, M., *My Ancestor was Jewish: how can I find out more about him?* (Society of Genealogists 1983).

Leary, W., *My Ancestors were Methodists: how can I find out more about them?* (Society of Genealogists 1991).

Milligan, E. H. and Thomas, M. J., *My Ancestors were Quakers: how can I find out more about them?* (Society of Genealogists 1983).

WILLS

Camp, A. J., *Wills and their Wherabouts* (Phillimore 1974).

Gibson, J. S. W., *Probate Jurisdictions: where to look for wills* (Federation of Family History Societies 1989).

Gibson, J. S. W., *Wills and where to find them* (Phillimore 1974).

WALES AND SCOTLAND

Hamilton-Edwards, G., *In Search of Scottish Ancestry* (Phillimore 1972).

Hamilton-Edwards, G., *In Search of Welsh Ancestry* (Phillimore 1986).

Whyte, D., *Introducing Scottish Genealogical Research* (Scottish Genealogical Society 1984).

MONUMENTAL INSCRIPTIONS, NEWSPAPERS AND DIRECTORIES

Collins, L., *Monumental Inscriptions in the Library of the Society of Genealogists, Part One: Southern England* (Society of Genealogists 1984).

Collins, L. and Morton, M., *Monumental Inscriptions in the Library of the Society of Genealogists, Part Two: Northern England, Wales,*

Scotland, Ireland and Overseas (Society of Genealogists 1987).

Gibson, J. S. W., Dell, A. and Medlicott, M., *Militia Lists and Muster Rolls* (Federation of Family History Societies 1990).

Gibson, J. S. W. and Mills, D., *Land Tax Assessments* (Federation of Family History Societies 1987).

Gibson, J. S. W. and Rogers, C., *Poll Books* (Federation of Family History Societies 1990).

Gibson, J. S. W. and West, J., *Local Newspapers 1750–1920* (Federation of Family History Societies 1989).

Gibson, J. S. W. *Quarter Sessions Records* (Federation of Family History Societies 1991).

HERALDRY

Burke, Sir J. B., *The General Armory of England, Scotland, Ireland and Wales* (1884 and reprints)

Fairbairn, J., *Crests of the Families of Great Britain and Ireland* (1860 and reprints).

Fox-Davies, A. C., *Armorial Families* (1929 and reprints)

Moncreiffe, Sir R. I. K., Bart, and Pottinger, D., *Simple Heraldry* (Nelson 1953).

Papworth, J. W. and Morant, A. W. W. *Ordinary of British Armorials* (1874 and reprints).

EMIGRANTS/IMMIGRANTS

Begley, D. F., *Handbook of Irish Genealogy* (Dublin Heraldic Artists 1984).

Begley, D. F., *Irish Genealogy: a record finder* (Dublin Heraldic Artists 1987).

Currer-Briggs, N. and Gambier, R., *Huguenot Ancestry* (Phillimore 1985).

Hawkings, D. T., *Bound for Australia* (Phillimore 1986).

SURNAMES

Reaney, P. H., *The Origin of English Surnames* (Routledge and Keegan Paul 1980).

Journals and Magazines

Computers in Genealogy (monthly), Society of Genealogists, 14 Charterhouse Buildings, Goswell Road, London EC1M 7BA

Family History (quarterly), Family History, Northgate, Canterbury Kent CT1 1BA

Family History News and Digest (six-monthly), Federation of Family History Societies, The Benson Room, Birmingham and Midland Institute, Margaret Street, Birmingham B3 3BS

Family Tree Magazine (monthly), 15/16 Highlode, Ramsey, Huntingdon, Cambridgeshire PE17 1RB

Family Twigletts (bi-monthly), Family History Club of Great Britain, 19 Penybryn, Mountain Ash, Mid-Glamorgan CF45 3TJ

Genealogists' Magazine (quarterly), Society of Genealogists, 14 Charterhouse Buildings, Goswell Road, London EC1M 7BA

The Scottish Genealogist (quarterly), Scottish Genealogical Society, 21 Howard Place, Edinburgh EH3 5JY

Most overseas genealogical societies publish their own magazines. Some addresses are as follows:

The Society of Australian Genealogists, Richmond Villa, 120 Kent Street, Observatory Hill, Sydney, NSW 2000, Australia

The Genealogical Society of Tasmania, PO Box 60, Prospect, Tasmania 7520, Australia

The New Zealand Society of Genealogists Inc., PO Box 8795, Auckland, New Zealand

The New Zealand Family History Society Inc., PO Box 13.301, Armagh, Christchurch, New Zealand

The Genealogical Research Institute of New Zealand, PO Box 36–107, Mocra, Lower Hutt, New Zealand

The International Society for British Genealogy and Family History, PO Box 3115, Salt Lake City, Utah 84110–3115, USA

The National Genealogical Society, 4527, 17th Street North, Arlington, VA 22207–2399, USA

The British Columbia Genealogical Society, PO Box 94371, Richmond, British Columbia, Canada V6Y 2A8

The Ontario Genealogical Society, Suite 253, 40, Orchard View Boulevard, Toronto, Ontario, Canada M4R 1B9

The Quebec Family History Society, PO Box 1026, Postal Station Pointe Claire, Pointe Claire, Quebec, I19S 4I19, Canada

The West End Family History Society, PO Box 760, Florida 1710, South Africa

INDEX